Who I've Become

Unmask the Treasure Within

©2010, 2013, 2017 by Sonya Visor
3rd Edition
All rights reserved

All scripture quotations are from the Holy Bible, NIV and King James Version.

Covenant House Press, LLC
Racine, WI 53403
www.covenanthousepress@yahoo.com

ISBN-10:0984354123 (Print Version)
ISBN-13:978-0-9843541-2-2 (Print Version)
Published in the United States of America

Cover Artist: Melissa Talbot
www.itsmelissatalbot.com

Interior Design: Susan Harring
harring87@att.net

Books by Sonya Visor

Inspirational
Who I've Become

I'm Coming Out, With My Hands Held-Up High
(Forthcoming Title)

Non-Fiction Anthologies
Love. Hope. Faith *(Who Shall Save Me From Myself)*

SistahFaith *(My Own Creation)*

Blended Families (The Check for $3.96)

Fiction
Love Me For Who I Am - a novella

Got to Be Real *(Forthcoming title)*

Make It Last Forever *(Forthcoming title)*

Let's Drink To That *(Forthcoming title)*

Fiction Anthologies
All I Want For Christmas *(Unwrap the Gift)*

A Time of Praise: Christmas Anthology *(Giving You the Best of My Love)*

When She Loves *(Taken)*

Dedication

This book is an offering unto the Lord God Almighty.
It was the touch from God's hand,
the whisper and confidence of His Love that
has caused me to be free to bleed and heal before Him.

Today I show my scars to many because
God has given me the liberty to take off my mask.

Thank you, Heavenly Father, for saving
my soul and saving me from myself.
Who shall keep me from falling?
The Lord, strong and mighty!
I dedicate this book to You because
it is You that made me who I am.

Who is the King of glory? The LORD
Strong and mighty, the LORD mighty in battle.
Psalm 24:8

Acknowledgements

T o my best friend and the man I honor, my husband, Tony Visor. I can say that I am still in love with you after twenty-five plus years. You are my true love, the kind that has romanced, healed and helped deliver me from my wounds. I am so thankful for you.

The godly covering that you are to our two sons and me is amazing. You, sweetheart, are a support system to me all by yourself.

Baby, you have watched me come full circle with this project, and you stood by my side through it all. You are heaven sent. How else would you know how to love me through this time, right when I needed you most? You, my man of God, were ordained to help birth the person I have now become. I am TruU because God used you.

My son, Tony Jr., that day you were sent into our living room to save me was the day God activated the seed of evangelism in you. You are a lot stronger than you know. Be authentic in God. Jason, you are so special to me. A son who is blessed; God sees the best in you. It is our prayer that we have instilled the love of God in both of you. If you have God, you have everything you need.

Want Free Books?

Don't miss out when Sonya has her give-a-ways! To be notified of new releases and when she's giving her books away for free, please consider signing up at her website: www.sonyavisor.com

Got 2 Minutes? Free 2-Minute TruU Videos

What's all the talk about TruU? What does it mean to unmask? How to embrace who you are? Check us out, as we talk about TruU topics and tips to help others become free. Visit and click the thumbs-up and subscribe to our Be Unapologetically TruU Channel. #Listen #Receive #Laugh #Love #Cry #BeFree

Join The TruU Community

Join us on Facebook and be a part of the movement! Share, discuss and Be Unapologetically TruU! #Motivation #Inspiration

www.beunapologeticallytruu.com

Who I've Become

The Treasure Within

By Sonya Visor

TruU
Books

Covenant House Press
Real ♥ Raw ♥ Risqué ♥ Inspirational Books

To my family, I couldn't ask for better parents. Mom and Dad, you two are the best! You have always encouraged us to aim high in life and to do so with integrity. Thank you for being good examples. I am a daddy's girl, but a mommy's girl as well.

My sisters, Regina the protector; and Cheryl the jazzy one, you both are beautiful inside and out and a fan club all by yourselves. You know how to keep it real so that you can love somebody else right where they are. You two are the best sisters! To my prayer-warrior-friend-sister Roshena, you know too much about me and yet you still love me. Now, that's Christ-like. You have prayed me through too many situations to count, and you've given me the truth when I needed it…even when I didn't want it. I thank God for the prophetic call on your life. It's who you are—so embrace it, while shaking the haters off! This is a God-thing. Get ready, TruU has gone international!

I have too many literary honorable mentions to name, and I don't want to forget anyone. I am thankful for all of my Sister Scribes and people who have helped me along the way. Thanks for keeping me accountable and being an inspiration with my many writing projects.

This shout out goes out to Makasha Dorsey! The woman God used to help me transform this book. I had already felt the nudge to update the book, so I prayed, and God led me to this beautiful soul. It's rare to find someone who helps unselfishly. God used Makasha to transform *Who I've Become* into a ministry tool. The blessing is she had read the book and talked about how it had blessed her. For her to partner with me to upgrade this book was surely God ordained. I am thankful for her skill, insight, and ability to be in tune with my heart. Nothing but God! More importantly, for being a vessel of God to confirm this ministry of unmasking buried souls.

I want to give a shout out to my Saturday Morning VCM Bootcamp Scribes. This class was ordained! Your input and talent helped polish this book. You all are amazing writers and I can't wait for God to make your names greater with the gift He has given each of you.

Felicia Murrell! You are exactly what the authors said you were—great! Your ability to connect with an author's voice is powerful. You are definitely gifted, sharp and easy to work with, such a blessing - exactly what I needed for the finishing touch.

Credit for the beautiful book cover goes to my nieces, Dominique Overstreet and Ashley Conley. They are fabulous! My awesome-unique photographer, Jennifer Dallman captured the photo. I appreciate the time all three of you gave to this project. A special thanks to Mary and Regina for being there for me. ☺ Your heart to see what God was doing humbled me. At the end of last year, I had a vision of my book with a new cover. I tip my hat to phenomenal graphic designer, Melissa Talbot for the eye to encapsulate what I was trying to convey with the book cover. Masking comes in many faces. Thank you, Susan Harring for partnering with TruU from the beginning in 2010. You are a gem, a true treasure.

To you, the reader, **God bless you** for investing your money and time to buy and read this book. It is my prayer that you will receive encouragement as you digest the pages of *Who I've Become*.

Blessings and Be Unapologetically TruU Always,

Sonya

Forward

I had no idea when I met my wife that I'd be on assignment. It's a funny thing about an assignment; it's a task given for a specific purpose. I did not know it at the time, but I was birthing my wife into her destiny, her ministry, and her passion. My wife had been dealt some bad circumstances, especially with extended family. Hands that should have protected her had touched her. I married her over twenty years ago, fully understanding what had happened to her, but not fully comprehending how to deal with her. Enter God! The Lord started to show me how to minister to my wife. He dealt with me in detail so that I could deal with her delicately, although there were times I had to be tough. She was going through changes in her life. Masking played a big part in her life. I saw who she had become, who she was and where God wanted to take her—so I pushed, I pulled, and I encouraged her to simply be who she was. In doing that, she had to confront and deal with self-esteem issues, uncertainties in her life and all the dark places that had her to the point of trying to take her own life. I didn't fully get what had brought her to this place, but I did know how to pray.

My wife finally made a decision to take off the mask and be transparent in the presence of the Lord, and she got delivered. She has experienced firsthand what it is like to not to be the person you are called to be, but her deliverance has been awesome. I am so proud of her for recognizing that her past does not dictate her future. Now an author, playwright, and pastor, her life is marked by transparency. She knows what it takes to get free. I encourage you to embark on my wife's journey and see if something said can bring healing in your life. I will tell you the truth, I didn't know that we both were on assignment because Sonya has been a blessing to me, living this message before me: Take off the mask!

In the Master's Hands,

Pastor Tony

Table of Contents

Chapter One
INTERRUPTED—HOW I BECAME

～ॐॐ～

"Are you having sex?"

"Uh…no, Mama. I'm not having any sex," I said, darting my eyes from my mother's gaze as I fidgeted with my school bag.

"I keep washing your underclothes, and I do not like what I'm seeing, Sonya. It looks to me like you are out there having sex with somebody!"

My mother was demanding an immediate answer. Here was my gate, my huge opportunity, to get this heavy burden off my shoulders. But I was scared. How could I explain all the wetness and discharge in my panties at age eleven? After years of being touched, fondled, and squeezed, my body was now responding to the very thing I hated—the touch of his hands. And I sure couldn't tell my mother that it was people we called … *family*.

As my mother's voice escalated, I'm sure the neighbors received an earful. "Sonya, you bet not be standing up here in this house lying to me!"

My mother stood there fuming while I remained quiet. I wanted to speak. But, the words... The words I needed to say should never pass the lips of an eleven-year-old girl. The words I needed to say screamed in my head then lingered on the tip of my tongue as I stood there with my eyes averted, feigning interest in the brown shag carpet that covered our living room floor. The words I needed to say stopped lingering and formed one solitary thought: *You should know who's touching me.*

I couldn't talk like that. Not to my mom. I was raised in the old school way that commanded respect to elders, especially your mother, and that would not allow me to disrespect her. My emotional frailty had nothing to do with her. So, there I stood impassive, as if I were a statue, trying not to move or blink to keep my tears from flowing. *This is our secret,* he would say...every time he touched me, every time he took from me. For five years, I kept his secret.

I couldn't tell a soul, not even my mom.

"I tell you what! I'm making an appointment to take you to the doctor. Then we'll know."

14

I could have worked the streets as a prostitute at nine years old if it were left up to the hands that touched my body and changed my life. When most little girls were jumping rope, playing with dolls, or learning to braid hair, trusted family members abused me. Yes, several family members took advantage of the trust that comes with blood relation. My mother and father entrusted their most precious gift from God, their little girl, to family members who only saw value in my passive personality and femininity.

A man, who had to be in his late forties, introduced me to things no child should ever have to experience. And, my uncles perpetuated the torment. They were people who were supposed to love and protect me. Instead, they touched and fondled me. They taught me how to lie.

I should have told my mother the truth that day. Unfortunately, those same hands that explored my body served as an invisible muzzle. Their lies and perversion silenced and imprisoned me, creating cracks in the secure foundation poured by a mother and father who had a pure love for me. The abuse caused me to distrust my mother's ability to feel my pain and protect me. I believed the lies of my abusers and feared their wrath.

Threatened with the penalty of poor treatment, I kept my mouth shut and my head down. Standing before my mom, I transformed into someone I didn't like. I put on a mask. Inside I was far from the loving, caring, truth-telling, strong daughter my parents raised. I became something less. A perfectionist at wearing a mask.

15

I tried to be perfect. I couldn't allow anyone to see the pain, hurt, and confusion resting on me at the hands of my respected, beloved family members.

Trouble and shame pursued me. The transgressions of those who violated my life created scars that bled over and over again with each new incident. What was there about me that allowed them to mistreat me? I wanted to know what drew these people to me. What gave them a right to touch me? When they put their hands on me, they changed my thinking and awakened my womanhood well before its time.

With my innocence tainted, my outlook on life changed. The wide-eyed fervor and excitement of childhood I once had no longer existed. How could I climb onto my mother's lap and tell her what happened to me? How could I accept my father's protective embrace only to whisper my hurts into his ear? I couldn't do it. So, I covered it up and wore the victim's garment of shame. I became a superb liar. I learned to hide the wrongdoings of my abusers even though I hadn't done anything wrong.

Fear paralyzed me. I was afraid to ruin my home and family by dropping the truth on my parents. A battle raged within. On one hand, fear and depression loomed inside of me. On the other, I still felt special because of my father's love.

While my abusers brought me down with sexual advances, my dad esteemed me and gave me a stable foundation at home. Naturally good people, my parents created a family environment filled with love and discipline. Both of them had a way of making

16

others feel comfortable and welcome, like old friends they'd known for years. They were my security blanket, and I didn't want to mess up the happiness in our home. I didn't want to cause problems because my parents had to work. Had my father known someone was touching me, he would have taken matters into his own hands. Instead of being my rock at home, I would have had to write and visit him in prison.

Then there was my mother, the voice of righteousness and reason. On one side, I was bound and essentially trapped by keeping my abusers from being found out. On the other side, I kept hearing my mother's voice saying, "Don't do this and don't do that." To put it mildly, I was conflicted. If my mother found out about my abuse, she would have been utterly outraged. As a child, I was mistaken to believe my mother would not be able to handle the truth. I didn't see a way to win—not with both sides pulling and tugging at my soul.

That's part of the reason why I never told anyone. I couldn't tell anyone without destroying what good there was in my life. So, I walked around and acted like all was well.

If I sent my abusers to jail, I would ruin their lives. The sad truth that they were already ruining my life escaped me. The lies were a pretense to hide reality, but the truth was buried deep inside—suppressed and tucked away, creating bondage in my mind, compelling me to right this awful wrong. I tasked myself with fixing a problem that I didn't have the capacity to create or repair. I realized that adults taking advantage of me, a child, was not my fault but my response to the abuse showed otherwise. Somehow, I blamed myself.

My carefully constructed persona of perfection was a byproduct of my victimization. I needed to cover up the things that were flawed in my life. My abusers obscured my rationale. In trying to be right and perfect, lying became second nature. Not only did I lie by omission about my abuse, but I also began to lie about other things—especially anything concerning school and friends. I became a professional at wearing the face that fit the situation. If my mother saw I was despondent and said something about it, I became happy. If I was quiet and somebody made a remark about my silence, I talked. I learned to adapt to please everybody. It was my way of avoiding any raised eyebrows. I felt safe being who I needed to be at the moment. I learned it from my abusers. They needed me to be a compliant, malleable girl and I became that.

To this day, I know why I kept the secret, but I cannot pinpoint exactly why I went along with the program for so long. I couldn't have asked for better parents. They would have protected me and given me the help I needed. But they couldn't do anything about something they knew nothing about. Fear and deception made me think lying was easier, causing me to tuck my true feelings in an envelope, sealed inside my heart.

As I look back, I realize God kept me from going insane. Often times, right before my abusers tried to take even more of what wasn't theirs, something would happen to make them stop. The phone would ring. Someone would knock on the door. My oldest sister seemed to always know when to call my name. By the grace of God, they fondled all the bases, but they never scored a homerun to obtain the ultimate prize: my virginity.

Don't get me wrong. The other stuff they did was more than enough abuse for a lifetime, but God didn't allow them to steal everything from me. My sister knew what was happening. She felt like she could do nothing to stop it—anymore than I could do. We were both trapped because my sister and I had to go to these people's house every day in the summertime while my parents worked. We were stuck.

THE FIRST TIME

"Sonya."

"Yeah, Sam?"

"Come on down here. I wanna show you somethin'."

I took calculated steps into the basement to see what he wanted, though nothing came to mind. Absolutely nothing. I drew a blank. *What does he expect me to do, look at the green paint peeling off the wall or all the clothes piled on top of the dryer?* I thought.

He knew I knew he didn't have anything to show me when I stepped away from him. *Awkward.* A feeling of foreboding warned me something creepy was about to happen.

He stared at my undeveloped chest. I wasn't even wearing a

training bra, but his eyes landed there taking me in like I had something to offer him.

I felt naked, uncomfortable. I didn't know how to respond to the attention or how to avoid Sam's piercing eyes. *Run*, my head told me. *Run back up the stairs and out of the house as fast as you can.*

Sensing my fear, Sam reached for my hand and stepped closer to me. "Where you going?"

"Uh...back upstairs," I said, fighting back the tears that burned my eyes.

"Stay here with me." Sam rested his arm on my shoulder.

I stood as still as a statue. The life and air around me stifled, as if, like me, it froze. The acceleration of my heart alerted me to danger. I didn't know what to do.

"You know you're my special one?" he said, his voice controlled and low.

"Yeah, I know. Sam...can I go now?"

"Yeah, in just a minute." I didn't move, but the arm draped around my shoulder tightened.

We stood there until Sam shifted his weight. His hand slipped from my shoulder to my breast in a matter of seconds. His hand stayed attached to my breast. I thought *what do I do? What do I say? His hand should not be there. Come on, Sonya! Think!*

I panicked. Inside, I cried. One tear. Two tears. An internal dam of secret tears filled my heart, and then the door slammed. Sam's hands stopped fondling and the child within stopped crying.

I shifted. *I can move again.* My heart rate decreased, returning to its normal pace.

"Hey, anybody seen Sonnie?" my sister asked, calling me by my nickname.

"Uh...huh...," several family members respond to Gina as she searched for me.

Here was my escape, my moment to break free. "Gina, I'm down here!" I yelled, wiggling out of Sam's hold. Free from him and my trance, I rushed past Sam and galloped up the stairs.

He called out to me, "Don't forget your money."

I hesitated. *I don't want any money from you.*

"Go on. Take it to the corner store and buy you and your cousins something."

Any other time, the money would have been a welcomed gift. I knew this time it was payment for my silence.

That day, I became an emotionally interrupted child. My life became that frozen, stolen moment in the basement with hands touching me where they shouldn't. A voice that pretended to love me while whispering lies into my ears.

The abuse didn't stop there. On days when we'd gather to watch television, I'd find myself stuck on Sam's lap for long periods as we all consumed sitcoms. There was nothing funny about my situation. I always felt awkward perched on his lap.

If only it had stopped there—with just him. I may have brushed it off with the passing of time and put the abuse out of my mind. Instead, my offenders multiplied and became bolder in their touches and kisses, sometimes undressing me, telling me to be still and to keep quiet while they did things to me. "Shhhh!" Over time, I got stuck on that same decision. Do I stay or do I go? It seemed to be my theme song. What does a child do in a situation like that? She plays along.

My abuser controlled me. If I wasn't obedient, he treated me poorly with the cold shoulder or, even worse, told my cousins not to play with me. When you're a kid, that kind of stuff hurts.

Our home, where my mom and dad provided a safe environment, became my ultimate escape. When my mother picked my sister and me up after work, I would dismiss the day's horrible events and enter my peaceful, safe place with her. Then, tomorrow would come, and the chaos started again. I acted as though nothing was wrong and got better at covering the truth. As I learned to adapt, pleasing everybody and warding off any negative attention, I focused on getting the spotlight off me. I stopped being Sonya and lost myself.

The emotional baggage seemed to spill over into every area of my life. I tried to control it, but this thing was way bigger than me.

Sam marked me. I believe neither one of the offenders knew what the other was doing. I believe each oppressor thought they had me to themselves. One abuser, in particular, was very demanding. This one, we'll call him Jimmy, introduced me to oral sex at age eleven. Afterward, he would send me back outside to jump rope with a promise that he'd buy me candy. What a disgusting deal— me fulfilling his sexual desire in exchange for a piece of candy?

My abusers planted seeds of shame in my soul with roots so deep it's a wonder I'm still here. The shame isn't what pushed me close to the edge; it simply delivered me to a place called guilt. Most people don't talk about shameful feelings and due to the dilemma my relatives put me in, I had no desire to share this anyway...*ever*. These grown men made me, a child, become their woman for their sick perverted desires. Did it not matter that I was a part of their family? I was kin. Who does this to their family?

TOO MANY HANDS

I left the bedroom, trying to control a very hard cry while keeping quiet at the same time.

"Sonnie, what's wrong?" my sister asked as I came outside and sat on the step. That was it. My mouth couldn't find, let alone form the words to answer her question. My tears escaped, and I wailed. No words. I had no words to express how used I felt. Tears tumbled down for the humiliation I had just endured.

As I cried, I could still hear Jimmy instructing me quietly, "Act like a big girl."

How do big girls act? I hadn't had my first "real" kiss, but he had me on my knees trying to perform an act that was foreign to me. *If this is what big girls do, I don't ever want to grow up.* I was grossed out beyond measure.

The encounter with him was the worst. I couldn't even hold up my head. *Does anyone know what I've done?*

I sat on the porch, crying and wondering, *why me.* My sister cried too.

My sister wiped her face and said, "That's it. We gotta tell."

After what seemed like an hour, I responded, "I know...we gotta tell."

But you know what? We didn't tell a soul that day. We figured if we could just get out of having to go to the caretakers while our parents worked, we would be free from further abuse, or so we thought.

My sister did her best to protect me. She'd call my name at just the right time most days, but she couldn't always be there to save me. Only one year older than I, to this day, watching out for her family is a strong trait of hers. If she senses trouble, she is there. It's like she is making up for not being able to protect us in the past.

Our approach to our abuse took different paths. My sister became the protector, and I tried to please everyone I could.

24

We were far from being free. It was only the beginning of a new chapter in our lives. All I had to do was go to my father or my mother, and they would have made everything all right, but I could not fix my mouth to say the words. The abuse was so bad, I had trouble myself believing that anyone would do this, yet they had.

My oppressors thought if they didn't penetrate me vaginally, then they weren't doing anything wrong. Their twisted thinking had ruined my own thought life. Regardless of what they believed, it felt wrong. How does one shake such things? How can you forget the abusive hands of an enemy, literally touching you and shaping your life in a painful way that will always be part of your past?

I didn't know, but I quickly found a way to help me deal with all of that. All that drama created something in me I didn't like. I noticed a very familiar, oppressive spirit or behavior about myself at certain times. I dismissed it since I didn't see how I could change it. I didn't know it then, but I know now—what I went through had a hand in creating my character.

I was emotionally sick. At a young age, I worried about things a lot of kids typically don't worry about. I felt like I was an object to be used, not a person. My emotional deficits were a direct result of somebody else's sin. The stain of their activities had rubbed off on me. On the outside, I mirrored a happy child so no one would see my pain. On the inside, I was crying out for help. But when you make a decision to live life out of a perception of how others think you should be, no one can see the true you—not even you.

Unmask (Think About It):

- Did anything happen in your life that altered you or your thinking?
- What was it?
- How did you deal with it?

Chapter Two

AND IT HAPPENED AGAIN

"Sonya, come here for a minute," Sam called from the doorway, interrupting the fun game of kickball I played with my cousins. He stole my laughter the moment he uttered my name.

"Okay. I'm coming," I said as I trudged to the door, hearing the request in Sam's voice. I never wanted what he had to offer, but he gave it to me anyway. I needed a miracle—the passing of one day without one of them calling my name. Without one of them touching me.

It seemed like a rain cloud stood over my head when I saw Sam gawking at me through the screen door. His blue shirt and sunglasses conveyed everything he stole from me: happiness and joy.

No one else heard the request in his tone, but I knew exactly what he wanted.

I felt strange and sneaky, but I still left my kickball game. It was a hot summer day. All I wanted to do was play with my cousins and friends.

Does anyone know what he wants from me? Does he touch the other girls? Every time we were all together, he only called my name. No one else was singled out. Surely, they hear the salaciousness in his voice. Like me, everyone present was a child. The only way they'd know what was about to happen is if their innocence was gone, too. Their innocence allowed them to continue playing kickball—something I wanted to do. While I had to accept Sam's advances—something I didn't want to do.

Maybe if I hurry, he won't keep me long.

As I approached the door, my legs felt like cement. I needed to tell somebody so this wouldn't keep happening to me. But who would believe me?

Lord, if you can hear me, please don't let him keep doing this to me. It doesn't feel right. God, you know I hate it.

"Hurry up, gal," he instructed.

I went inside.

Immediately, Sam closed in on me, shrinking the already tiny hallway. I felt like a caged bird that wanted to peck his eyes out. But, I was too scared to do anything, so I just stood there. He partially blocked the window by leaning his body on the door. The familiar fragrance of

Old Spice cologne filled my nostrils. His scent gagged me. I hated that smell.

The faint sound of my cousins' laughter taunted me. They were having fun while my heart thudded as my mind came to grips with knowing that Sam's hands would be all over me within a matter of seconds.

"Do you want some change to go down to the store?" he asked as his eyes roamed over my prepubescent body. He should have said Hey, girl. Can I touch your unformed breast and grind up against you for some change?

I didn't want candy money. I wanted Sam to stop touching me. To stop violating me. To stop sexually abusing me so I didn't have to keep lying. "No...uh...," I stuttered, "uh...that's all right." I reached for the door handle, but his hand covered mine. I froze. Yuck!

"What's wrong with you?" Sam's voice filled with accusation. "Somebody trying to give you somethin'."

I took the money. Knowing that by doing so, I was somehow giving him consent, but I didn't want him to get mad at me. I just wanted to get out of there in a hurry, and taking the money was the quickest way to get away from him. Where is my family? I need them to catch him. Does anyone miss me? Somebody, please call my name. I pleaded on the inside, knowing if I screamed he'd grow angrier.

"You know I care 'bout you?" His eyes roamed over my body. Thankfully, his hands had stopped.

"Yeah…I guess." Afraid to make eye contact, I kept my head down. I didn't want any of my actions to give him permission to do what he wanted.

He reached for his wallet and pulled out a few bills. "You are my baby girl. Don't tell nobody I gave you this money. It's all for you."

I wanted to scream, "I don't want your freaking money!" I needed my sister to come in and save me, to call my name and interrupt him like she always did. Every time my sister called my name, it meant I had a chance to escape. Through the gap in the window he wasn't blocking, I could see her now jumping rope with the rest of my cousins.

And there I stood in the hallway, with him breathing down my neck. I held my lips together and folded my arms, twitching like I had to pee. He didn't like it. He wanted me to be still. Gina, please call my name.

"Go on outside. Remember, you're my baby girl." He opened the door, and I ran like I had a mile to get to safety.

Another piece of me died. The numbness living just below my conscious grew. I wanted to block it out and pretend it didn't happen.

I knew my response was unhealthy, but I couldn't deal with the painful truth. I just thought, w*hew, I made it this time.* I knew it wasn't over for me. There would be a next time. There was always a next time.

If I had taken the "love" those men showed me as real love, I would have been more messed up. I was ashamed of who I was and what happened to me, but I knew real love. I knew abuse wasn't it. All I was to those men, those relatives, was just someone to use for their depraved pleasure.

Fortunately, I saw real love at home with my parents. The man in my life who loved me beyond measure was my dad. He never touched me in an inappropriate way. My dad gave me real love. It was safe. My father displayed normal love and affection for my sisters and me, and he showed genuine affection toward my mother. With no abuse suffered at the hands of my parents, I don't know how that perversion found its way into the lives of my sisters and me. But, it did. It invaded our safe world with enough power to try and destroy my innocence despite my parents' good example.

Time brings about a change whether we want it to or not. Abuse over time caused great change in me. I was old enough to know the truth and developed the "I am no longer a little girl" mentality. I suppressed my secrets enough to operate normally while my insides raged. After all, I was getting too old to be told when to stand still, get undressed, and do this and do that by my abusers. Yeah, that was the old me—a new day had dawned.

31

I often wonder how my life would have been if I had opened my mouth and told my parents from the beginning. I can't help but think about how many cousins I might have saved by breaking the curse of silence. I saw the big picture when it was over. Unfortunately, I was imprisoned daily through obedience to the voice of my enemies.

With my innocence gone, the solid foundation laid by my parents developed cracks. Eventually, those cracks overtook the strong, solid foundation my life was built upon. Negativity broke down what was once solid. I responded to this travesty the best way I knew how, by being a good little girl. Opportunities for me to tell arose, but I always succumbed to fear and kept my mouth closed. I thought if I told on them, I would be telling on myself. After all, they did pay me. I accepted what they gave. I'd never refused their advances or their money.

My mother, being the great woman I described, made good on her promise to take me to the doctor. Any good mother would want to know *why* their eleven-year-old daughter had acute *wet panties* syndrome. In my mind, the examination would provide her with concrete evidence that dirty hands had been caressing my stored treasure.

AT THE DOCTOR'S OFFICE

I sat in the waiting room next to my mother, waiting for my appointment. Between watching the slow hands on the wall clock and glancing at the tight line my mother's lips made, I restlessly anticipated my freedom. Finally, my secret would be set free. I'd be released from the misery each one of my abusers bestowed upon me.

As much as I wanted every secret touch and kiss to be revealed, I grew anxious at the thought of my mother finding out. What will she say? Will she be mad at me? Would she think I enjoyed it? A nurse called my name, interrupting my thoughts, and escorted my mother and me to an exam room. Moments later, a tall man entered.

"Hello. What seems to be the problem today?" he asked.

I fell limp as my mother cleared her throat.

"Dr. ...Uh," she cautiously began, "Sonya's underpants have been soiled. She has some discharge. But...she told me she hasn't engaged in sex, but, uh, that's what I need to find out today."

The doctor raised an eyebrow. "We'll take a look to find out what's going on with the young lady," he said nodding at the nurse who stood by the door with a clipboard in her hand jotting down notes.

I shifted in my seat, sensing that he had already decided I was, in fact, having consensual sex.

The doctor's gaze settled on me as he spoke to my mother, "We'll have Sonya get undressed and give her a full exam."

An awkward silence filled the room. I guess they were waiting for me to come clean before I got caught in my lie. I lifted my chin defiantly.

Yes, something is going on sexually, but it is not what any of you think. And, it is not mutual. You'll see. I'm ready.

He shifted his eyes to my mother, "Mrs. Brown, I would like to talk to Sonya alone for a minute or two."

I gently said, "You will see, Mama." A new confidence filled me because soon she would know I hadn't done anything wrong. At least...not willingly. The doctor would know. The shame would finally stop.

She left the room as she said, "Uh...huh."

The doctor fixed his gaze on me. "Now that your mother is gone, you can tell me the truth."

"I told you the truth."

Appearing frustrated, he responded, "Okay, Missy, in a few minutes we will see."

I sighed as he walked out of the room, then I changed into the gown the nurse left for me.

When he returned, he instructed me on how to put my legs into the stirrups. I just laid there and waited to see what would happen next. In a feeble attempt to get me to relax, the nurse told me what to expect and talked to me about random topics of interest. It didn't work. Pelvic exams

34

are invasive. It frightened me, but for some reason, I trusted these complete strangers.

"Well, my-my…" The doctor's confusion was evident in his voice. I smiled, thinking I had won the tug-a-war of who had some of me and who didn't.

I said, "See, I told you."

"I'm proud of you for telling the truth. You are still a virgin."

In a strange way, hearing those words made me feel whole again, especially after all those times I felt like washing my body until I couldn't wash anymore. What was on me that made these people think they could just reach out and defile me? Did I have an invisible sign above my head that read, *I'll let you use me*?

"You've got to tell my mother!" I said, needing my mom to know I was not having sex. I didn't want her to think I was some "fast-tailed girl," as she called it. No one had gotten my treasure, though many had tried.

The doctor announced to my mother, "Mrs. Brown, I am happy to say your daughter is still a virgin." Although my mother smiled, she looked worried.

My mom's visible worry knocked some of the air out of me. In that moment, I had a chance to tell her that although I was physically and medically a virgin, a close, beloved relative violated my body as often as he could. The discharge in my underwear came from all of the friction caused by the rubbing and dry-humping. But, I said nothing. That day, I lied to my mother—not knowing the collateral damage being a keeper of disgusting secrets can cause.

Five years later, I used another's hand to get what I wanted.

Partaking in someone else's sin made their sins become mine is how I thought for so long. Until a beautiful soul conveyed this truth. She said, "It may have felt like you were partaking, this is *not* true. Their sins, the wrong-ness, their violation belongs to them and them alone. Now, how you chose to respond or act out in life as a result of that perpetration is on you. But, you didn't willingly partake, you were forced. Two, their sins are theirs, not yours. You were a victim, not a participant. There is a huge difference."

UNMASK:

- What opportunity have you passed up to come clean, tell the truth or confront something?
- Why did you seize the opportunity? Or, what made you hesitate?
- How did you feel afterward?
- If no confrontation, why do you believe you are holding on?

Chapter Three
MAKING THEM PAY - TRANSITION

❦

By age sixteen, I recognized that I could take my power back from my enemies. I figured out how to flip the script by observing the behavior of my violators. I could mess with them and dish out things to hurt them too. They became jealous and overly protective of me. It sounds crazy, but it's true.

One particular abuser became profoundly disturbed by the attention I received from male friends. I wanted to shout in his face, "You are not my man, you are family! Don't you get it?" How could any normal person be angry at something that is natural in a teenage girl's life—like boys? Obviously, my perpetrators weren't normal. They interrupted my youth. I decided they could get mad and stay mad. They couldn't have anything else.

I became a quiet storm once the hands stopped finding their way between my legs. Over a year had passed since they'd commanded me into back rooms and bedrooms. The damage was done. I had changed. With my innocence gone and my trust depleted, vindictiveness arose within me. I had them right where I wanted them.

I seized the opportunity to become the user and relished in my ability to make them pay for using me. Now, I had power. They couldn't keep their hands to themselves, but I found a way to get even and get paid while still protecting my treasure, my womanhood. *You didn't get it before, and you certainly will not get to go there now that I am in control.*

If these men had no problem using me as a child, I had no problem turning the tables and using them. Once I was in the driver's seat, they walked in fear.

"Are you going to tell?" they asked.

"Sonya, I know you gon' be quiet," Jimmy whispered as he passed me in the kitchen.

"Mm-hmm, yeah," I said, walking away from him. He couldn't read me and never knew if I'd tell or not. Instead of paying to touch me, Jimmy now paid for my silence, tucking a twenty into my back pocket.

Gotcha! I smiled. *Now, you're afraid I will share with your church, our family, and the entire world that you are not the person you appear to be. You don't want anyone to know. I paid when you tainted my body, mind, and soul with your perversions.*

Even after the abuse stopped, they wanted me to keep quiet. I wanted to yell, "This lie is killing me!" Instead, I said to them ever so sweetly, "Your secret is safe with me. And, I need a few dollars."

That's how I got even. I allowed them to think I'd tell. I did this until I got to the point where I didn't want anything from them at all. For a while, it felt good to have the upper hand.

I saw enough movies and videos and read enough magazines to know the advantages of being a woman. I knew how to obtain what I wanted from a man. I had even seen women at church shake and use what God gave them to manipulate men. It was powerful to observe the use of feminine wiles in action. Using it to my benefit liberated me. Or, so I thought.

The lure, the conquest, and the tease of "what you could have" oozed from my mind and my body as I stepped into womanhood. I convinced myself no one could hurt me because I was in control. Hurting and using became my method of operating.

Capitalizing on their fear was a lucrative business. The power of my secret drove me forward, subjecting my violators to an unspoken truth. The secret screamed at my abusers every time they laid eyes on me. The secret, one that once made them powerful, now left them powerless causing them to spend their wheels and their money as they tried to figure out how to keep me quiet. The secret protected me from further abuse, setting me free from the heat of their hands. The secret was now a payday opportunity for me. Next time, maybe they'd keep their hands to themselves.

My mind adapted to this new way of thinking as a way of coping with the harsh truth of my abuse. It empowered me to know I could get what I wanted before giving anyone permission to touch me. It felt good to decide how far the touches and caresses could go.

And, even after I got what I wanted there was no guarantee I would let them touch me. My rules reigned. I taunted them with my actions. *Give me what I want, and there will be no problems. Guess you should have never touched me, huh? It sucks being victimized, doesn't it?*

From getting pocket change for school or a meal from McDonald's, I schemed and seduced my seducer with games and unkept promises. He spoke to me like we were a couple, but I knew otherwise. Initially, I allowed him to get a touch or feel here and there. It came at a price for us both. But, I knew I would never allow him to enter my special place.

My abuser became my bankroll and my chauffeur. Money for jeans. *How much do you need?* A ride to the skating rink with my friends. *What time do you need to be there?* If he didn't do what I asked, the threat of exposure met his ears. Exposure to the police held a greater weight. The risk of being locked up has a certain effect. During my teen years, you couldn't turn on the evening news without hearing stories about people revealing details of childhood sexual abuse. Fathers were being turned in. Uncles were unveiled and exposed for sexually abusing their family members. My offenders didn't know what I was going to do.

Due to the way my parents raised me, I felt a little guilty at times. However, the guilt passed when I reminded myself they had asked for this. I manipulated them the way they manipulated me. My anger grew when one of my abusers had the audacity to imply that he really didn't do anything at all to my sister and me. How was sexual touching nothing? That question led to others.

- Where did this all begin in our bloodline?
- Had someone hurt them first?
- Where did they get the idea that it was okay to hurt children?

Maybe it was nothing to them, but their sexual abuse messed with my head and my heart. Believe me, nothing but God could erase the damage done to me. No apologies were offered—not from any of them. Certainly not from me.

They should have been glad I wasn't pressing charges against their sorry behinds. I wasn't saved. I didn't know Jesus at the time. I didn't know about forgiveness or mercy. I responded in a way that would hurt them. I had been quiet too long. So, I behaved like the monster they created.

I was not created to be a monster. However, through years of emotional and sexual abuse, I was manipulated into being the opposite of the *fearfully and wonderfully made* creation God ordained. Silence should never have been the answer to their unspoken question, "Can I touch you and get away with it?" My silence spoke volumes, essentially giving them the green light to put their hands on me. And I spoke this permissible language often, without saying one word.

Silence spoke for me. It put me in a place that allowed me to accept such perverse treatment. If only I had broken the silence and acted. My abusers chose me because I was young and scared. My youthfulness appealed to them because they could control me.

My thoughts clanged loudly inside my head. I hoped somebody would hear my unspoken misery and see the signs.

Although I carried these games into my young adult life, I managed to protect my virginity. My mother instilled high values in all three of her daughters. Being whole in that way mattered to me. According to statistics, I should have been loose and promiscuous because I had the makings of someone groomed for sexual pleasure. To this day, I am not in the double digits when it comes to sleeping with men, not even close. I praise God for that. God protected me by not allowing my abuse to destroy me.

Looking back, I suffered more than sexual abuse. By all accounts, they made me a child prostitute, giving me pennies for something priceless. I was degraded, humiliated, and left feeling numb and unclean. Long hot showers couldn't cleanse me and perfume couldn't mask the stench of their bodies on me. I lived in constant awareness of repeated violations. I didn't do anything to deserve being handled like a hooker.

I didn't do anything to deserve being *used* and *abused*. The quiet storm inside me raged as I took what was mine with a vengeance. I became more damaging to me, yet I kept up the façade blending in like the chameleon they taught me to be. The mask I wore morphed even more. I was the good girl who manipulated others. Yes, I had a certain amount of power over them at the expense of losing myself. No longer able to recognize myself, I disliked the person I was becoming.

The mind is powerful in its ability to take you anywhere you want to be. That's how fantasies originate. When that same mind is tainted with dark places that hang on to you and surround you, it's like you are playing in the devil's playroom. To be removed from that kind of entrapment takes an act of God. I was going deeper and deeper into an all too familiar, dark place. In fact, the dark place became where I felt most comfortable. I took comfort in my secret misery. I settled into a place emotionally that I hated. That dark familiar place became home. It was what I knew, and it was who I had become.

When something is constantly on your mind—to the point that it alters your decisions and controls your every move—you indeed have become the very thing you don't want to be. For some reason, pleasing the enemy became more important than becoming clean. When your mind is messed up, you can't make sound decisions because your whole world is clouded by the thing that possesses you. It's like you're giving off an aroma that attracts the very things you neither want nor need. It pulls you away from the negative behaviors you need to correct and cements you into a person who is standoffish, preventing anyone from knowing the real you. Not dealing with the truth, keeping secrets, and covering sins all come together to create a dangerous, hard ground in which the devil cultivates. I made my home in the center of rocky, unyielding, good fruit destroying soil.

The more I suppressed the pain and the shame, the harder I became. By age twenty, I carried the weight of the world on my shoulder. I did a great job of covering up what I didn't want anyone to see, but keeping up the act cost me. There were only a few people I let my guard down with, but I never felt totally free. I was afraid of what somebody might see if they looked close enough. I wore a mask at all times. I rarely felt safe enough to let the real me roam free. In survival mode, I masked my thoughts, fears, and desires to avoid questions and stares. No one could see my pain or my shame.

Like most people, I searched for something to make me feel better. I started to discern who was right and wrong for me, steering clear of people who meant me no good. I didn't want to deal with anyone else who would bring darkness into my life. I'd lived in the dark long enough.

The positive changes in me brought about accusations from relatives who should have known me. Instead of seeing the truth that I held on by a thread, they accused me of being stuck up. *Sonya thinks she's better than us. That's why she's standoffish.* Early on, I realized pleasing people was impossible. So, I withdrew.

It's funny how no one notices when you're going through life-changing problems. When you start making positive changes, however, those close to you don't know how to respond. Out of their own fear of change, people become judgmental or critical instead of helping. While their meddlesome nature would have been appreciated when certain male relatives were victimizing me, they went on with their lives pretending there were no issues in the first place. I was the one with the problem. I held on to my sanity the best way I knew how—by keeping inquisitive and whispering devils off my shoulder.

Certain family members saw but didn't see. A few had to know. One blamed me for her grown husband abusing me. She pretended as if she didn't know, but she had to have suspected something for her to treat me poorly as she did. She said I was fast, that I tempted and provoked her husband. Instead of accepting that the man she married was perverted, she chose to hate me. She knew the truth. A child can't tempt a righteous man to sin.

These people weren't distant relatives that spoke against me. Close family members accused and ridiculed me. If my mother had known the truth, the script would have changed years earlier. And, I fear someone would have had to bail her out of jail.

I couldn't believe they blamed me. The only logical explanation for their inability to accept the truth is they knew something and didn't want it to be true. I cried rivers of tears. It didn't change a thing. Like me, they chose a lie over the truth. My abusers knew how to manipulate children and adults. I was there. I knew how it all began, and it wasn't what they chose to believe. After hearing crude names come out of that relative's mouth, I separated myself from that side of my family. I needed to hold on to some semblance of sanity.

I was seriously tempted to round up some 'hood friends who would have slapped this woman silly to teach her a lesson. Victims should never face blame. But, that's what she did. I felt sorry for her. Her husband was a pervert who molested children. I imagined how awful she would feel if she admitted that she had chosen such a man as her husband and lover. I realized her response was actually out of the pain she must have felt regarding the truth. In the face of her own rejection, she sowed seeds of discord to cope with her pain. Once again, I remained quiet.

My silence came at a greater price. She tolerated her husband's adulterous sin and other perversions. Eventually, others fell prey to his lures.

To admit you need help after someone has mistreated, rubbed, touched, forced you into things, talked nasty about and sexually scarred you is a humbling experience. In addition to worrying about the pain caused by my abusers, I fretted over what people would think of me if I ever shared my story. My silence was the easier road, yet it was killing me to walk it.

Often misunderstood by those who should have taken the time to know me, I carried burdens too heavy to shoulder alone. I was way too serious all the time, always pondering things to the extreme, becoming overly analytical and obsessive about what had happened to me. As I moved away from making my enemies pay for their sins, I entered a downward spiral. To everyone around me, I remained poised. I wore a mask to protect my pain. I believed the lie that life was all about appearances and the exhaustion from riding an emotional rollercoaster finally began to take its toll. I could no longer hold it together.

I grew tired of explaining myself and my dysfunctional view of life to females while protecting myself from their men. I lived life based on who I had become and not who I was created to be. In reality, I was an emotionally bleeding woman in hiding. People responded to what I showed them. I let them believe what they wanted to believe instead of letting them get close enough to understand me. I retreated because I could not trust anyone.

When you practice something long enough, you get good at it. I wore my mask well, but I was tired of the chronic turmoil in my heart. Daily, I gave an Oscar worthy performance of the perfect girl who had it all together. On the inside, however, I wrestled with not wanting to be the cause of drama in anyone else's life. As I entered into my twenties and started working full-time, all the things that happened in my past up to that point were constantly in the back of my mind. No amount of masking would make them disappear. Those things had become a part of me. They created my dysfunctional world and affected my choices.

Things are never as they seem. I appeared to be normal, but I was far from it. I felt like I wore the scent of sin. I found myself trying to mask it with a smile or by attempting to be 'just fine,' but my dysfunction had escalated to the point where I couldn't even stand myself. I am surprised I didn't develop an eating disorder or drug addiction because at times I was overwhelmed and needed something to feel better. I kept trying to be perfect, but I only made a bigger mess of things. I understand why some people suffering from abuse cut themselves to let the pain out. I wasn't about to go there, but I was bleeding inside.

People respond differently to things, even though they may have endured the same incident. My ultimate goal was to keep the imperfections buried, but I discovered you just couldn't cover up something bigger than you. Eventually, the pressure blows up in your life and spills out like an erupting volcano. All I wanted was to return to the peace I had known in childhood before abuse marred me. The peace I cherished and shared with my immediate family was what I needed to survive and to heal. But, I was way too busy guarding myself so no one knew what controlled me. My pain ruled my life from behind the scenes. My attempt to make them pay rendered a payday for me that could have destroyed my life.

M.I.N.D – ME IN NEEDLESS DISTRESS

Shame not only covered me, but it carried me from one bad point to another. It accompanied me to a place where my heart ultimately thought of death as a solution to get rid of the intense pain. How in the world could I break this dysfunctional cycle, this rollercoaster ride that I carried with me through school into my teen years, and on into my adult life? One minute I'd be doing well and the next moment, I'd experience depression or sadness. I had to move on. I had to flip the script or I'd cancel out every good thing left in my life. I was trying to hide their sins to save face for them…and for me. I had to think outside of my normal zone and my circumstance to get my life back.

I fought this battle most of my life. Perfectionism ruled. I had masks for everything. My acting made me lose even more of me. My abusers had stolen my identity, and I needed a complete makeover. I needed a Savior to find me. The enemy's hands held my mind captive. *Who else knew? Was it my fault? Why on earth had they chosen me?* I didn't know the answer to these questions. But I knew I'd take my secrets to the grave.

It became evident that I wasn't responding in a healthy manner to the abuse. Masking my pain led me to make the wrong responses in normal, non-abusive situations. Instead of wearing masks to hide my pain, I wore masks to hide my errors. Hiding became all consuming. My enemies' hands, ones that had not touched me in years, still directed my life behind the scenes. I couldn't admit when I was wrong. If I did, the floodgates would release everything I hid.

Like a harsh stain, the distress permeated every area of my life. I was running from what I had become—a shameful young woman motivated by guilt to cover up the truth.

They say actresses are divas, and I understand why. Wearing different faces and being someone other than your true self is utterly exhausting. I didn't want to wear masks anymore. I didn't know what to do, but deep down inside I knew I needed to do something different. The time had come to give each one of my oppressors exactly what they deserved.

UNMASK:

- How do you see yourself in this chapter?
- What captivates your mind? What do you think about excessively?
- What causes you to feel drained?

Chapter Four
IN THE CHURCH PEW

⟨⟨~⟩⟩

This can't be my life became a constant lament as I died on the inside. I moved from mad to distant. I kept my pain on the down low—wearing a mask that covered my soul. I didn't know who I was anymore.

Lost, I continued going through the motions of life. I had to figure out—someway, somehow—how to let go of my past, but the work was too much to bear alone. I pushed the pain down and forged ahead, not knowing failing to face my problems would elevate them. Every time the pain or shame tried to reveal itself, I covered it with the mask of perfection. Sonya, the independent, did a great job at appearing to stand on the outside. No one knew I was falling over on the inside. Crying out loud, sometimes screaming within my soul, I stayed in that desperate place far too long.

I needed something more. I knew I couldn't go on living in functional depression. Wrestling with these unwanted feelings discouraged and overwhelmed me. I simply couldn't deal with it.

My internal strength waned like a tiny boat tossed on angry waves. I took a perpetual emotional beating while it appeared as though no one else had problems. I knew they had everyday worries about the failing health of loved ones, the economy, crime, and politics but none had my soul-destroying kind of problems.

A life built on secrets, guilt, and shame followed me, hovering over me like dark rain clouds about to burst. Whether I acknowledged them or not, these were my unwanted friends. Volatile and brooding like a summer storm. My frenemies—Secret, Guilt and Shame decided to throw a party. Suicide, a special guest, came with bags. She needed a place to stay. A life to end.

My life was as good as any. I was perfectly groomed to sacrifice myself.

Suicide gave me the promise of freedom from my pain with her sweet, deadly whispers. *"Go ahead and take your life. You can't make it through this. If you kill yourself, you won't hurt anymore."*

I listened. The solution in those lies tempted me. *You mean I could make the pain go away and stop the suffering?*

I didn't want to die. I wanted the pain to leave. I wanted the guilt to stop weighing me down. I wanted to stop obsessing about my abuse and my abusers. I wanted freedom from oppression. I wanted my heart to take joy in beating, to soften (Ezekiel 36:26).

I went back to the church to find peace. Unfortunately, what I found were the same people I left. Imagine sitting next to the individual who used, abused, and accused you. Imagine if they carried on, mere feet away from you, playing the role of *the good*

Christian. Every "Amen" and "Bless the Lord" proclamation they shouted made me reel. They praised God, not taking one thought to the abuse inflicted nor the consideration to apologize. They lived a double life as they always had. One even had the audacity to tell me I needed Jesus.

Self-righteousness doesn't allow us to see our sin. It causes us to condemn others (Matthew 7:3-5).

I wanted to shout in his face, "I guess I do need the Lord after being handled by your nasty self!"

Every curse word I knew wanted to come out of my mouth in full force, right there in the church. God gave me control despite myself. I ignored my enemy and pursued my healing. I sought God even as Sam sat across the aisle watching my every move. One Sunday, defiantly, I returned his gaze. His embarrassment made him turn away. Maybe God was working on him, too. But, I wasn't there for his benefit. I needed a touch from the Lord.

The hypocrisy extended beyond my family. We had our problems. So did everyone else. On several occasions, I found myself sitting next to the wives of men who were actively pursuing me. Yes, these supposedly God-fearing men sought ways to dishonor and break their marriage vows. It was even more disheartening to find the wives at church were no different than my family members when it came to their husbands. Instead of handling the problems they married, they became angry and contentious toward me. They thought I wanted their men. I couldn't believe they had their hands in the air praising God after treating me in such ugly ways. I had my issues with residual and lingering sin, but how could these people possibly judge me?

There were a few genuinely good believers in God's house. Had it not been for them and people like my parents, I don't know if my deliverance would have come when it did.

Surrounded by people wearing *Jesus Saved Me* masks to cover up living like hell in private, I fought for my blessing. *How can hurt people ever get free if someone who's just playing church blocks real, authentic connections? How can hurt people get help if hypocrites are the gatekeepers? We say the doors of the church are open, but who is standing there to greet us?*

God is. He will supply everything we need and more if we focus on Him instead of those around us. I'm thankful I knew my deliverance was in God. I knew my heart, the organ that had suffered the most damage, was safe in God. He was my answer then and remains my answer now.

For every person who said, "You don't need to be here, you're a lost cause," there were several others who compelled me to come back to God. To keep coming back to church.

Keep coming, sister. The doors are open wide to all who seek His face.

We often get discouraged when we encounter hypocrites. Remember, God didn't tell us to seek their faces. They have too many faces to seek with all the masks they wear. Seek one face: the face of God. He doesn't change (Numbers 23:19).

I sought God in spite of the hypocrisy around me. If I couldn't go to the house of God, where could I go?

It wasn't long before I found myself walking down the aisle to meet Jesus. I tried to stay in my seat. I thought *maybe, next Sunday*, but I felt a tug and a pull drawing me closer to Him. The preacher gave an altar call, and I put one foot in front of the other and made my way down the aisle. The pastor led me in the sinner's prayer, rejoiced with me, and then turned me loose to go back to my old life with a new spirit inside me.

It felt good to be free. I was excited and scared at the same time. There are no words that can fully express how I felt that day. I felt deliverance working in me. The dark and oppressive spirit had been lifted from my life. I felt God's love. I knew He was real. I'd taken the first step and received Jesus Christ as my personal Savior.

After I left the altar and went back into the world, I returned to my sinful ways. I had no one to walk beside me on my new journey, and I didn't know how to stop nursing my pain.

IN AND OUT

For a season, I would show up at church on Sunday morning to sing in the choir at the 11:00 a.m. service after stepping out of the bar at 2 or 3 o'clock in the morning. I was confused, wondering about God's purpose for my life. Clubbing wasn't it. Even when I did all the right things, it was for all the wrong reasons. Inside, I was as far from an angel to my family as I could be, but I looked like one on the outside. This act got old real quick. I was the apple of

God's eye, and He was preparing my heart to trust Him for complete deliverance and healing. In the midst of all of my mess, God was there. I went to the altar every time I messed up. I was never told I needed to do that. I just knew I needed to get clean.

I remember walking down the aisle three times at church to get saved. Nobody told me all I had to do was repent in my prayer closet before God and it would work the same as in front of people. Instead, they watched me repeatedly walk down the aisle like a fool after the first salvation prayer. I was searching for help, and the church almost missed it. They sat there in the pews. Some even snickered as I made my way to the altar—again and again. I guess they thought I was a lost cause or maybe they thought they were better than me. I truly felt many of these people were embarrassed for me.

This is my opinion, but I have no idea why they would be embarrassed as they sat in the pews and watched me humbly go forward to seek forgiveness. I was the one walking down the aisle with all eyes on me. I felt their negative thoughts, heard the mumbling, and saw some of the members' countenances change as I made my way to the altar. They probably thought, *please not her again*, or maybe the organ player just wanted to close up shop for the day because I was holding him up. I don't know what people were thinking. I can only tell you how I felt. What I do know is: I wanted to be right with God and didn't know what else to do but go to Him…over and over again. He held the answer. That much I knew.

One Sunday morning, I stood up in church after being moved by the Spirit. I felt God's presence touch me. Soon after, the Holy Spirit convicted me. That conviction caused me to cut some things and certain people out of my life.

OH, BUT WHEN THE TRUTH CAME...

Church service was over, but I remained seated after a weeping episode at the altar. Why? I couldn't tell you.

I buried my face in my hands to get myself together.

As I gathered my purse, Bible, and coat and prepared to leave,

someone tapped me on my shoulder. I turned, and an older woman with the biggest, brightest smile I had seen in a while stood before me. She lifted my spirit because her smile exuded love and concern for me.

"Baby, can I talk to you for a minute?"

I nodded, knowing it was a rhetorical question. This woman of God seemed intent on sharing with me.

"Baby, this thing is between you and God."

I just looked at her, searching, trying to figure out what "this thing" was that she spoke of.

She continued, "You need to quit coming down here to this altar—you saved." She nodded for emphasis, all the while holding my gaze and my hand.

A weight I didn't realize I had been carrying lifted. I felt lighter as if a burden had been released. *This is what I needed. Thank you, God.* All the talk I had heard about surrendering your life to God made sense now. I was thankful someone had finally told me I didn't need to get *re-saved* each time I sinned.

Tears flowed. My reaction was so intense, it took a few minutes for me to compose myself—again. The older sister in Christ took me into her arms and hugged me as the power of God's love flowed through me.

"I'm saved," I sobbed. I had no doubt despite all my mess, I was truly and irrevocably a child of God.

The words the woman of God spoke that day ended up changing my life. Her powerful admonition sent me in the direction I needed to go, but I still didn't know *how* to live right. I was saved with all of my stuff from the past still in my memory giving me signs and feelings from yesterday. They weren't in my face until I got home where they met me at the door. Memories of things and people from the past came out of nowhere to remind me of my sin. I had to battle the memories, but it was nowhere near the heaviness that I had before. Now, I had help, a place I could go—my altar.

I made the mistake of doing what many new believers do. I tried to ride on the emotion I felt without doing anything to keep my faith strong. I failed to read my Bible or pray consistently. Because of this, the spirit of suicide lingered in the background, waiting to come back and torment me if this "Jesus thing" didn't quite work out. How could someone who can't give life ponder taking it?

The real drama began when I tried to maintain peace by breaking ties with a relationship that only meant me harm. I had a run-in with the law as a result of my attempts to please people, but that's a book for another day.

At the time I didn't know enough to go before God to release the pain and build myself up. I would make my way back to the dark, familiar places. Not consistently, because I was no longer comfortable being there.

Progressively, things got better. I experienced deeper healing and began to see life differently. Things were looking up. But then, even though I hated it, I'd travel backward and revisit the past. The behavior was like a dog returning to its vomit—gross, but a compulsion that can't be resisted.

Love found me in more ways than one and took me to another season in my life. In this new season, I had to battle with myself while being pulled, kicking and screaming from sitting in the back of the church to sitting in the front row. Honestly, I didn't know why the Lord would do that to me. But as sure as He is God, He did it, even though I cried and hollered, "Not me, Lord!" The Lord had a plan for my life. This plan was something I didn't daydream about, wish upon, or have any aspirations of ever seeking. Never in my life would I have thought I'd become the first lady of anybody's church, let alone the first lady of a church I took part in founding. The Lord truly set me up and caused me to fall in love. God blessed me with this man. The truth is I didn't deserve his love, but God gave him to me anyway.

Even as I work in ministry today, I never ridicule young men and women who can't get it together. There are some who club all night on Friday and Saturday and struggle with sin the rest of the week, but show up to church on Sunday. I know if they keep coming and saints keep praying, God will move in their lives. Those bonds will break. That's what God did for me.

People were interceding on my behalf when I wasn't strong enough to do it myself. Satan knew God had a call on my life. From the very beginning, he tried to stop me. But God took what Satan intended to destroy me and used it to help me minister to other women. He placed a good work in me (Romans 8:28).

UNMASK:

- Have you ever sat in church yearning for God to show up?
- What poor experiences, if any, have you encountered at church? How did you get passed it?
- Do you desire a relationship with God by accepting Jesus Christ as Lord?

- If you have done this, how connected do you feel to God or is something still missing?
- What truth have you heard to turn your life around?

Chapter Five
IT WAS A SET UP

We all have that friend who is constantly persuading us to do something. This one particular friend tried for weeks to get me out of the house and into the nightclub. Tired of hearing her mouth, I finally gave in.

Yeah, I said the club. The Lord was still working on me. Besides, I had been off the dating scene for a while, trying to do right by growing comfortable with myself in the absence of men. Not only had I turned down my friend's efforts to hang out, I was also rejecting dates with decent, available men. I wasn't looking for anybody and had placed myself in the no-man zone on purpose.

When my friend and I got to this club, I tried to get back into the flow of things. I was saved, but it's not like I had forgotten how to get down to some good music. Every time someone asked me to dance, I would send them over to my girlfriend. I was there because she invited me, but that was it. I had frequented this place before. It was nice and all, but I was no longer the same person. I was there to shut my friend up, not to "hook up" with or meet a new man. I wanted my friend to have a good time, so I smiled and joked around with her. Being engaged in light conversation about music and the people we watched kept her from asking me if I was okay. Having a good time with my friend was enough.

Eventually, the DJ did the last call and played one of those *end of the night* songs to help shut the club down. The first bars of *I Like* by Guy played through the speakers. *No, they didn't just play my song.* Listening to the melody, I knew I wouldn't sit that dance out. A guy had asked me to dance a few times, so I did. Not because of him, it was the song.

When the song ended, I left him and proceeded to the front door of the lobby. There, I waited for my girl to catch up with me. She was her usual slow dragging self, but I continued to wait, listening to the "go-home" music. It sounded good to me because I was more than ready to go home. I wasn't paying attention to anyone, especially after dodging the guy who wanted to dance. As I stood there, I noticed a guy sizing me up. *Caught ya!* I thought. He continued to talk to his friend, but I could tell he was trying to figure out if he knew me. You know the drill—checking me out on the sly. I stopped, posed, and stared at this perfect stranger.

Okay, I did more than stare. I smiled like somebody had paid me to smile at this man. That wasn't like me. I could play coy with the best of them. And, I was at the club to hang out with my girl, not to smile at a random good-looking man who checked me out on the sly. I was on a break from men. But, my interest had me looking like some young girl who'd just stepped off a big yellow school bus.

"Stop staring, Sonya," I told myself. I was exhibiting poor behavior. This connection was not supposed to take place. However, I could not stop staring at this man.

He must have felt my eyes on him because he turned toward me. I felt like a fool. This man saw me standing there without the decent home training my mom taught me. Thankfully, he smiled back and slowly headed my way.

Oh, no! I thought and walked away. And, bless God, he followed me.

That's how it all began. There I was minding my own business at the club. I wasn't looking to run into anybody, especially someone who would impact my life.

He found *me*.

SET UP #1

Who was this man the Lord sent my way? I can tell you this. He changed my life.

I promise you, I don't know what caused me to plant myself there at the entrance of the club or to gape at this man. Divine Connection, maybe? But I am so glad I did.

When I came to myself and stopped acting like a crushing schoolgirl, all I could do was an internal headshake and walk away. He followed me and told me his name was Tony, but we never exchanged numbers.

When I came back to myself, the walls came back, too. Back then, almost everyone's number was in the phone book. Eventually, I got myself together and found his number. I'm so glad I *let my fingers do the walking* to call him. We began to chat and date regularly. I slowly became the lady I was trained to be. I can laugh aloud at that now, but I'm so glad I called him. I should have given him my number when he asked me for it.

When he found me, he was drawn to me as I was to him. As we learned more about one another, my walls began to crumble, and I started to become this new, unveiled Sonya. His realness made me want to take off my mask. This man didn't change faces or personalities to get what he wanted in life. Never once did Tony show me a false appearance about himself and it allowed me the freedom to be the fearfully and wonderfully made Sonya God created me to be. He spoke a foreign language I wasn't accustomed to, but one in which I quickly adapted—no hidden agendas. It is what it is. He was saying, "I am who I am." He was a good example to me. To be your truest you at all times is essential. And for me, it was a goal.

The real test of authenticity happened when Tony met my parents. He did not change who he was in front of them. He remained free to be himself. I even brought something up that I tried to convince him to do previously before meeting my parents, thinking for sure he wouldn't say no. He simply said, "No, we are not doing that." *Doesn't he realize that he is standing in my father's living room?* I thought as Tony's unabashed *no* sank in.

My mom is a hard sell, and even she agreed with my dad when he said, "Now, that boy is real!"

Tony was—and still is—solid as a rock. He is stable. Even though life had dealt him some hard issues, he knew who he was, in and out. He was in the very place I wanted to be—constant and secure.

We would talk for hours. Someone was interested in who I was as a person. In turn, I began to discover myself. Besides my sister, Tony was the first person with whom I shared the *entire* painful truth of my childhood sexual abuse. His response was totally different than the first male friend I tried to confide in. Tony embraced me as I gave account after account of the incidences that changed me. He was infuriated and wanted to wring the necks of my abusers, but knew it wouldn't take my pain away nor would it erase the past. In such a short period, we were being knitted together by God for a greater plan than either of us had ever imagined.

God used me to bring Jesus Christ into Tony's life. Imagine that! And God used Tony to sharpen and challenge me to be my true self. Remember when I said I didn't need any man in my life? Tony changed my mind because he spoke to my heart with sincerity and authenticity. I listened to him, and he listened to me, creating a bond that took us straight to the altar. After dating for six months, Tony took my hand, got down on bended knee, and asked me to marry him. I felt honored to be the bride of this handsome, chocolate man.

SET UP #2

Our life together blossomed and grew in the Lord. We were truly blessed and became one. In our first year of marriage, we added a son, Tony Jr. to our family. I found myself worrying if family, friends, and outsiders would want to know if I was pregnant before walking down the aisle. Then, I figured it didn't matter. I knew the truth. We were married in August of one year, and my son was born in August of the next year, so all they had to do was the math. There was ample time for a child to grow in my womb after the wedding, but it still wasn't enough proof to stop the crazy thoughts about what people would believe. Seeds of worry stirred up within me fertilized by my painful past. The ever-present history that made me doubt my decisions and myself was the same history that made guilt stir up over the dumbest circumstances—things I knew weren't even true.

My husband grew leaps and bounds in learning the things of God. As the Lord taught him, he ministered to me. Eventually, he announced to our world that God called him into the ministry. But man, did he have to tell everybody? Don't get me wrong, this was all good, and my heart was excited for my husband, but I knew what it meant for me. I was selfish because I didn't want to rock the boat. We were a good Christian couple, doing just fine until God revealed His plan to take us deeper. If my husband's life had evolved, then I knew life would change for me as well. I didn't want this to stir up my insecurities, but I knew it would. I was just getting settled and loving life fully for the first time. We attended church. Our marriage was solid. Everything was good. I had finally come to the point where I could control the pain from my past, or so I thought, but still things were great.

I made up my mind not to get in the Lord's way. I found out a long time ago that being in the Lord's way is not the place you want to be when God is working. Like any good wife, I supported my husband in a way that was biblical. My heart's cry was, "Take me wherever you take my man, Lord." Except, all I wanted was a *saved* husband not a *preacher* husband. I just wanted someone to go to church with and pray with, not the fishbowl life that came along with being married to a pastor. God set me up to make some major changes in my life. But I was determined to be right there, standing by my husband's side despite my discomfort.

I continued to read the Word and pray in preparation for this new role God had planned for me, but the thoughts of my past resurfaced. Satan was messing with my head again, and my focus turned from God to me, my past, and my pain. I didn't feel right being in the role of a minister's wife. I had too much of a nasty past for that, yet God wouldn't let me go. I started to mope around and ponder all the things God delivered me from as if they were still hanging around my neck. This was the last thing I needed to do. Negative thoughts from my past came forth daily because of what I chose to meditate on. As a man thinks, so is he (Proverbs 23:7).

Godly people often say that your past is your ministry. But, I was like whatever, God. I wanted to escape my past, not relive it. I didn't want to rehash my mess of destructive behavior, perverted folks, and crazy family members. My salvation was supposed to free me from this, not put it in my face and say, "Here I am. You still need to deal with me." I was so wrong. I resisted because I knew I'd have to relive things I had suppressed for years. I had to walk through my valley of buried issues, but it meant reliving those secrets. I would have to bring them up and deal with them to gain true freedom from my past. What kind of God allowed this type of grief to happen all over again?

I was floating way out there in the middle of the lake, shaking in the boat as the storm swirled around me. Like the apostles, I felt like saying, "Lord, don't you care that I might die?" But the Lord responded by showing me that mercy and grace were there the entire time. He was preparing me for what I would have to go through to be birthed as a new creation in Christ or renewed into the place I was supposed to be all along.

6∞∞∞9

Everybody knew the calling on my husband's life. I could see it clearly. The titles of Pastor and First Lady would be our new names. With those titles came the spotlight and the bar would be set much higher for us. Let us not forget the wardrobe inspections, which started immediately. Isn't it ironic that man tends to critically look at the outward appearance when God compassionately looks at the heart? Maybe it was easier for the people of God to analyze our clothing than to search their hearts.

This transition meant my seat in any church would change from the back row to the front row—permanently. To this day, over twenty years later, I've moved from despising to disliking the seating arrangement. I had only one thing I could help people with and that was my ability to relate to the wounded and not look down on others for their sins. I could love them right where they were because I experienced what God had done for me. Instead of allowing the sunshine to warm my face, I concentrated on and allowed clouds of despair to fill me. Thoughts like *you can't be the first lady because of your past and God can't use you* bombarded my soul. At that time, I would have rather died than go through the mental torment. The nagging thoughts of fear of oppression came and stayed. I needed Divine Intervention so I wouldn't have to face my fears alone.

UNMASK:

- What could you relate to in this chapter?
- What life adjustments altered who you were?
- How did you adapt?

Chapter Six

GOD SENT AN ANGEL—MY SON

O ur church life was drastically altered. Thank God my husband didn't want to be a minister in title only. He truly desired to walk upright. He had zeal, and we encouraged each other along the way. I shared my heart with him, but I was careful because I didn't want to burden him too much or allow his zeal to be dampened by my inner turmoil. After I shared a little bit with him about how I was feeling, he looked at me and sincerely said, "Why don't you just be you?" My pastor husband is such a good man. He said all he could ask of me was to be myself—nothing more and nothing less.

It was a relief to know he didn't expect me to be perfect or like other minister's wives. Especially with all the other nonsense people were trying to tell me about the role of a pastor's wife and what they expected of me. The comical part, if it weren't so serious, was that the commentary came from women who were never in the role of a pastor's wife and never would be. They could set the bar out of reach because they'd never have to jump over it themselves.

TIRED OF CHURCH!

We continued to grow stronger as my husband began to preach and branch out in ministry. I noticed people didn't want to hear that you had "bad days" and that revelation troubled me. At church, everybody looked all put together, whole, untouched by the evils of life as though they had never gone through anything difficult. Being on the inside of ministry and observing on a few occasions, I would see people become unveiled in the house of the Lord. But, for the most part, we all just seemed to follow suit and put on masks with our Sunday best. I knew these people needed the Lord to intervene and do miracles in their lives, but often I watched them come to church and leave the same way they had arrived. Why not come to church for prayer? We don't want individuals to know our business because they will see our flaws and question our faith. We cover up the true hurt in our lives by wearing masks.

Of course, you can't tell everything about yourself without discernment. However, the house of God is supposed to be where we are to come and ask for help. Each time I attempted to share my feelings of discouragement and depression, someone would say, "Girl, you got to trust the Lord," or "Just keep praying and things will change." And I'll never forget this one: "You got to have faith," ending it all with, "You are blessed and highly favored, Sonya!" All the clichés, but no manifestation of the Living Word.

I knew all of that. I just wanted somebody to help me deal with the issues of my heart, to go through the storms with me and support me. Aren't Christian women supposed to care for one another? Where's the vessel that can hear the cry in the wilderness? The cry of my broken heart needed to be released. I hoped someone would see my wounds, allow them to bleed and be soothed and healed by the Great Physician. I needed somebody to tell me to cry out, not say, "Shh" or "Hush, girl, you always crying." Could they not discern there was a reason for my grief?

After I got tired of hearing all the latest church jargon, I hopelessly hid the truth about my pain because clearly there was something wrong with me. Everybody else was *okay*. At least that was what Satan wanted me to believe. They talked about me at church functions.

So, I did what I always did. I embraced my immediate family and tried to find solace in their acceptance. I wanted to give them the stability I didn't have. I pushed against the grain of giving up and found myself in another place. I was screaming for help so I wouldn't sink back into the dark place I had come from, but no one could hear me. You and I both know it isn't normal to think thoughts of death while laughing at a joke. That voice screamed on the inside, but I couldn't reveal my hurt to anyone. After all, I was being trained to become First Lady. I had no other choice but to keep the pain to myself. A First Lady must be strong, solid, and astute. She has to smile and be welcoming. It was back to the patterns of the past. Like always, I kept my mouth closed. However, I would soon learn that silence was not the answer. Silence speaks lies and causes others to respond incorrectly.

Even though I was in that dark place that sapped all of my energy, I pushed myself to act the part of the happy Christian and arrived at church on time. Being late has always been a pet peeve. I did this Sunday after Sunday, looking good on the outside. I talked, but nobody heard me. I was there, but no one saw beyond the mask. I walked into church, ready to pray for my sister, but there was nobody there to pray for me. How could they not see the cloud of darkness hovering over my life? I mean it must have been there because I could feel it. It seemed like I could sense the presence of death surrounding me. It was the familiar, dark place of suicidal thoughts that I had known once before. It sought to devour my spirit and end my life.

I don't know how others crossed the road of suicide—or how they even got there in the first place—but it was looming in the back of my mind, especially during this stormy part of my life. There is no doubt in my mind that death has no racial preference. Whether you are white, black, Hispanic, or Asian, death doesn't care. Nor does it care if you are rich or poor. It wasn't my time. But, when you call for death to come before the appointed hour—my God— you know then that you are operating out of your will and playing right into the devil's hands.

That burial site on the inside of my soul kept shuffling and awakening skeletons as I went through the church motions. I'd suppress the pain, knowing those thoughts weren't right and that they could eventually overtake me. This went on for about a year.

The devil wanted me to give him a foothold. The last straw came when I lost my job. I didn't fully understand how much I cared what people thought of me until I'd gone through that period of adversity. It seems crazy, because losing a job is nothing compared to being handled by countless hands, but losing my job was the one thing that tipped the scales and sent me over the edge.

SET UP #3

I was at my lowest point, ready to do the unthinkable. Having a man of God wasn't enough for me to want to live because a marriage doesn't make one complete. No one but God can complete us. He knows what we need. God knows us better than we know ourselves.

I didn't just jump up one morning and decide I would commit suicide. That seed was planted long before I had the first thought about ending my life. How could I be so desperate to think that way? I was at the bridge of death, not knowing whether heaven or hell awaited me, and truth be told, I didn't care. I was deceived. To prefer to die and risk going to hell is a powerful lie from Satan, and it had its grip on me.

My job was as much a part of my self-worth as anything. From my perspective, losing my job diminished my self-worth. How I lost the job made me an emotional mess. Covering other people's sin had once again become my sin. Sonya, the do good, hard worker got fired. Worried about what people would think, I wondered if they believed the report about me. I was concerned about how people would view my husband if his wife had a poor reputation. We both knew not all church folks walked in love. I was a head case, to say the least. My husband being a preacher and well known by many didn't help.

I felt guilty for not being able to contribute financially to our household, although Tony told me not to worry about it. A helper by nature, not being able to help my family tipped my emotions toward devastation. I was always willing to give help but not able to receive it.

Something dark and ominous settled upon me, nearly overtaking my soul. I couldn't hear my spirit man anymore. My pain started to dictate what I was going to do or what I felt I had to do to change things. If I wasn't praying or reading, I was crying about my life.

As I look back, I recognize I had given away my power and become demonically oppressed and overshadowed. Darkness feasted upon the table I set. Suicide was the enemy whose focus is always to get the person in agony to pull the trigger and take him or herself out because the enemy can't do it. In all of my praying, I only heard God say one word: "No." I asked, begged, and pleaded for God to take what I was feeling away, and He simply said, "No." I didn't

76

see the revelation of God's answer until later. I had every detail worked out.

Every day, I waited until Tony left for work, and then I would throw myself a grand pity party. I pretended everything was all right when Tony was around and played the role of the happy wife. This often prevented him from asking if I was okay. Obviously, my husband sensed something was wrong, but I kept lying to him to make him stop asking questions. It was all about me—how I felt and how I saw things, contrary to how God would have us. Even though I didn't see clearly, I thought I had a firm grip on my actions. I still knew how to cover up, but Tony knew something wasn't right despite my insistence that I was "fine, just fine."

There had to be angels watching over my son because I was in the house, but I wasn't present at all.

My husband interceded on my behalf. I saw my husband off every morning with a smile, and then I would get back into bed. But, something in me was purposed to search the Word of God. I was looking for verses that mentioned that the Lord was merciful. I had learned at an early age how to grab hold of the Word and use it for comfort. This time, it truly saved my life.

Even though I read the Word of God, darkness still loomed, waiting for the perfect opportunity to take me out. I would settle in the living room with my clouded mind, literally on my knees, shifting from one couch to the next, crawling around on my living room floor crying before the Lord. Tears erupted from my soul. I don't know how I ended up in a fetal position, but suddenly that's where I was. I wanted to die. I still don't know how I was able to be in the Word with all of this darkness around me. I know today it was God. At that time, I couldn't see the light or the truth of the matter. All those years of abuse finally surrounded me, causing me to bow down in defeat rather than lean on God.

On the floor next to the couch, I found myself reliving every memory I thought was gone or at least suppressed. My past emerged in all its ugliness.

Two rape attempts I experienced as an adult came back to me. I'd hidden the memories in the dark corners of my mind so I wouldn't remember the evil in my oppressor's face every time I saw him.

All of the things in my life I didn't want anyone to see were right there staring me in my face—vivid and painful. The enemy purposed to use this to destroy me. I begged God once more to take away the embarrassment, the pain, and the overwhelming shame, but the Lord whispered, "No." It was something I had to go through, even though I didn't want to face it. I didn't think I could make it through all the trials, but I had to stare the ugliness of my past in the face.

"Lord, why do I have to feel this way?" I asked.

I had worked so hard to cover it up, but I couldn't hide from myself. I stood naked and exposed in all of my pain. This evil that wanted to destroy me had made me ready to leave my husband, my child, my mother, my father, and my sisters to find relief. All I could think about was stopping the pain. I could only see one way out—

death. I told myself it would be better for everyone if I were gone. This way I could spare my husband and my son any shame or pain that I lived daily. Of course, I did not think about the pain I would cause them if I left them by my own hand.

Just when I had made up my mind to do the deed, I heard my son. I hadn't done anything to startle him, and he didn't know what was going on inside of me. Tony, Jr. ran into the living room as a little messenger of God. I had unfurled myself a bit to a semi-fetal position when four year old Junior came in and called my name, "Mommy!"

I looked up. There was an angelic glow about him that day, a countenance of the presence of God. It was like one of those messengers from God we've all seen in movies. The Spirit of God upon him mesmerized me. I continued to stare at him. Once he was confident he had my full attention, he reached for my hands, and I felt a current. It reached out and touched me through Junior. There was a charge, and it wasn't a surge.

My son proceeded to speak life to me in a childlike manner. In my interpretation, he said, "Mommy…God loves you and so do I."

His words vibrated into my soul and the ripple effects will last forever. From the mouth of babes comes wisdom at the most unexpected times.

My spirit awakened, shaking me loose from the pit I dangled over, and the floodgates burst open that day. Tears of release flowed from me: grieving went, shame went, depression went, fatigue went. It all left me right there in the midst of my outpouring of grief. Every covered up and suppressed stronghold fell from my life. The chains of depression no longer bound me.

I didn't realize my son was still holding me until I had finished snotting and messing up his cute little sweater. He was smiling a glorious smile. In fact, he never stopped smiling. The Lord also smiled on both of us that day. Things have never been the same since. I often declare, in every situation, that I will live for the Lord and NOT die.

How could I have thought about such a thing as taking my life? Life was not that bad. Looking back, I can see how darkness had enveloped me. If I had willingly died with my son in the house, it meant I had totally given my power over to the enemy. What if my husband had found me? If my son had not come in or if another scenario had occurred, I don't know what I would have done to myself that day. What a sick memory I would have left taunting my family. All I could hear was my voice before God delivered me.

To this day, I am still rejoicing that the Lord sent deliverance in the form of my son. I know it was God that rescued me. Saying I love you was not strange in my family. My husband and I said it to each other daily. When my parents and I talked, we finished our conversations with "I love you." My sisters and I can't even go on vacations with our husbands without calling the family to share our love. We had no problems with showing affection to one another. Sharing our love was normal behavior.

The miracle was that my son could not hear without his hearing aids at the time. They were sitting in my bedroom because I didn't want him to hear me crying while he was playing. But he heard the voice of God. There was an anointing on him so strong that it broke the power of darkness in my life. I was just about to agree with the enemy that I needed to die, but love showed up and rescued me. I had to make a decision right then: life or death? I decided to stand up and face my demons. I pressed through all of those dark emotions. I saw that it wasn't that bad. I was free because Christ set me free.

The spirit of suicide hasn't rested on me since. Praise God! The power to resist the devil was within me all along—given to me by God. The Lord always makes a way of escape. This time, my friend, I will build my life on the promises of God. This time, I will see my future and not dwell on my past. My sin was allowing my feelings to take me into a place that could have sentenced me to no return. My sin was not trusting in God, the one who made me, to deliver me from evil.

I know now that God will take me where I need to go in life, and I can face life with Him at the helm. Is there anything too hard for Him? No. In all of my imperfections, I have come to this conclusion: whether I am at home, at work, sitting in the front row, in the back row, or even standing in the pulpit of the church, I can choose to believe what God says in His Word. During the tests of this life, I will stand strong, influenced by the hand of God and know who I am in Christ.

Jesus is an authoritative source. The source.

In the midst of darkness, the utterance of that name will make the devil back up and cease fire. If you are feeling depressed, doom-and-gloom, like life is trying to suck your last breath, it's time to sound off the name of Jesus. There's *power* in the name.

Love *in* the name.

Deliverance *in* the name.

Healing *in* the name.

Victory *in* the name.

Look at it. **Call** it what it is. **Deal**.

It doesn't matter if you are married or single. God knows the road you've traveled. He is not surprised by what you've been through. He can handle it.

Invite Him into the situation. If you can't say anything to anyone because you don't trust them or no one is around, say the name Jesus from your heart. If you can't find or form the words, *please* say "Jesus" until it moves your soul or moves darkness from around you.

Have the words but can't speak them out? Journal, prayerfully write it down. This has been an effective tool for people who have gone through the unmasking process. Attend a women's group that talks about what you've gone through or make a call to help centers at churches or crisis centers that will walk you through your emotions.

From experience, getting the issues up and out of your soul is the breaking ground for your new life. If the secrets stay in, they will win. Up and out is key. Evict it all from your soul. Breathe in new life and allow it to take up residency.

God will begin to orchestrate some things. Don't be afraid. Move in the direction God is leading you. I won't lie to you. It will be uncomfortable because these are unchartered waters. Keep moving.

You are going to have to look at this thing. Look. Once you see it, pause. Raise your head up and boldly stare at the situation. See it for what it is. You can't change it, right? Okay, now you've got to let go. Own your portion, but prayerfully release it all to God.

If you don't look, you will act like it's not in the same room with you, as if there's no issue. We both know you've been hauling the issues around on your back far too long. If you look, you will deal with it. God will show you how to defeat it and take back your power that's been there the entire time.

UNMASK:

- Have you ever experienced a dark time in your life?
- How did you get through it?
- As you reflect on this time in your life, are there any unresolved places?

- What can you do to bring closure or healing?

Chapter Seven
EVERYBODY HAS A MASK

People wear masks to hide their pain and protect themselves from being hurt. We all have donned masks for one reason or another. I am not talking about the minor incidents in life. What I'm referring to are those things that are tucked away, causing internal damage. These are the things that war against us and cause us to hide behind an alternate version of ourselves.

Adam and Eve hid from God in the garden, and people still struggle with hiding from God today. We try to hide the things that bring us shame such as our sins, our secrets, our fears, and, sometimes, even our dreams.

At a young age, I learned how to put on the right mask by watching others. When I was growing up, I watched the church women put on their happy faces to hide their tears. I watched them come to church—with or without a husband—pretending all was well while it was clear they were lonely. It was obvious to me, even in my youth, that after doing something as desperate as sleeping with a trustee or a deacon to get some relief from the loneliness, those ladies couldn't or wouldn't tell anyone about their pain. They still held their heads up while being used or becoming users themselves.

I saw how most people played the game. They thought nobody knew their stories. But, I watched. Through observation, I learned how to hide the true Sonya from the prying eyes of others. My experiences were my own. Some things you just have to keep to yourself.

Sometimes people don't know how to respond to vulnerability in others. They'll either brush it off or respond incorrectly. People with personal information might view a transparent person differently. Sharing can cause more pain when we irresponsibly tell another's secrets or use their circumstance against them. This could impact their ability to be effective at home, church, work, or in the community.

All I had to do was go through the motions of playing church, and no one would know the difference. Nobody needed to know the awful truth. If you want to know about wearing a mask, go to a church. I enjoy church and getting together with God's people, but that's where I mastered hiding in plain sight. As an adult, I didn't feel the need to tell anyone what I had done the night before or how sorry my life truly was. I never let myself be real with my brothers and sisters in Christ. To be honest, they couldn't handle the truth back then. And still today, some don't want to deal with the truth.

Both men and women fear being judged, criticized and rejected. If people were to know the truth about them, they would be open to judgment. It becomes easier to cover up the ugly things by lying or simply not acknowledging the truth. If there is a mask, the wearer's intent is to masquerade, to parade around as someone she is not, to impress while not dealing with the issues causing her to wear the mask in the first place. The wearer takes on a new persona and identity. It's a stolen identity.

When a person chooses to live like this, who can truly know them? Stolen identity is presenting a false version of you. You choose another's identity or create an identity that suits the person you'd rather be. You are a counterfeit. You wear an identity that portrays you like someone else, someone other than your true self, and it is not *your* life. Sadly, most of the time people do this for what seems like good reasons. Think about it. Would you *intentionally* pretend to be somebody terrible? No way! Most of the time, we are reaching for more confidence, money, beauty, or position. Most folks don't fantasize about becoming people they think are losers. We want to be better than who we believe ourselves to be.

People see material possessions or status and draw conclusions about who they think we are based on those things. On magazine covers, we see couples that appear to be in love who are miserable. On talk shows, we hear guests tell us how to live a better life when, in reality, their lives stink. We watch Christian networks and think the messages are for everyone else, not us. How can we be better when we are not comfortable in our skin? Sadly, this is not just what we see on television or in magazines. Too often, this masking hits very close to home.

Masking is hard work. A person takes on a new identity because the individual does not like what's going on deep inside. We end up ignoring the flaws we wish to hide. Instead of dealing with those flaws, we allow them to fester, and they get swept right into the soul. Covering up old soul wounds creates painful tears that rip us up inside. Because those wounds were covered, confronting or dealing with the circumstance and making way for healing is often accompanied by continued pain and discomfort.

We are totally different people beneath our masks; people who act out roles far from our realities. The goal of wearing the mask most often is to deliver the message that, "all is well," but we forget all masks have holes and they can only cover up so much. The very things we wish to suppress often leak out through those holes into our lives.

Before I delve deeper into this topic, let me make it clear: we all have some business that we must keep to ourselves. I'm a realist, and I know you can't be out here in the world telling things only you and God should know. So, please be careful where and how you bare your soul to avoid further damage to your mind and spirit. But there are things that if unveiled will liberate us. You should be free of long-held secrets that torment you. Letting go of the past—

actions, hurts, regrets—will bring you one step closer to the real *fearfully and wonderfully made* you.

Revealing the real you, or becoming unmasked, is a challenge. It is threatening. Masking creates protective walls. It feels comfortable and secure behind those walls. There, you don't have to be accessible. Living behind certain types of walls give you the illusion of false safety. When the walls are up, they block any interruptions to our created "norm." But, that norm is not real and wearing the mask comes with a high price. The hardness that overtakes our souls just keeps on getting harder. Suicidal thoughts, drugs, depression, abuse, and a myriad of other things, the pain has many faces.

Deciding not to mask requires us to look at and confront the source of our pain. Doing so dismisses and breaks open the false securities that took root when we looked the other way and chose not to deal with our problems. For years, this is just what I did. Victory begins with taking off the mask. I admire people who say, "That is how it used to be for me, but this is where I am now." Only a small percentage of those who mask will ever reach this place.

So many people will continue to choose to get up every day and go through life dressing the outside, making sure every hair is in place, ensuring they are dressed to the nines. Never, ever forgetting that mask.

Their souls will bleed from the pain of being covered up for so long, unable to heal or breathe. They promise themselves they will keep all imperfections and problems out of sight. They believe being covered—inside as well as out—is best for them. And that's the lie because masking is bondage due to the restrictions the mask creates. To be free from restraint is to live in truth, to live *your* truth.

A woman we will call Linda experienced exactly this liberation when she unveiled herself at church. I'd like to share her story.

Linda didn't care what others thought. She was known for selling her body, drug abuse, and child neglect, but the day she testified, she opened her mouth against all the odds. The people in the church gave her the attention her demeanor commanded as she spoke boldly. When she finished, we all realized how much courage it took, courage some of us knew we didn't possess, even in our salvation.

The young lady walked to the front of the church and stood at the altar waiting to receive permission from the pastor to share her testimony. She told all of her business. Now, as discussed before, we are not supposed to do that. We must make sure we find safe places to bare our souls. Unfortunately, in front of the whole church isn't always a safe place.

Still, I envied this woman because she knew that we, the people, the church, didn't have the ability to set her free. God was her only help in her time of trouble. He and only He can pull us from the grave.

Linda spoke with such freedom that she shamed all the pew-sitting judges who were ready to cast stones at her in the house of God that day. She ended her testimony, declaring these words, "You may know where I've been, but it's up to God where I'm going!"

She cleared the house by setting the record straight. She boldly told us her truth, and it spoke volumes. When she opened her mouth with such candidness, she inspired others. She chose not to cover up her sins any longer. By calling her sin what it was, she took away its power over her.

"You don't know my story," Linda said. "You think you know me, but you only know what I've done. You know about the sin, but you don't know about me. My sin doesn't define who I am."

It's a new day when you can take off the mask. When that happens, help has a way of finding you.

What would people think if they knew the truth about you? Somebody reading this book needs the freedom in that very thought. You know who you are. You can't leave home without putting on "the face." It's key to looking like you have it all together. God forbid if the world knew about the real you. But what if they did? What is the worst thing that would happen? Would it be so bad? What you don't realize is that even through the façade, people will glimpse your despair and pretenses. You might say all of the right things, but intuition tells those around you something is not right. What then? Maybe they'll get involved, learn all your secrets and help you turn things around? Or maybe they'll make one of those dreaded judgment calls that led to your cover-up in the first place? Unbeknownst to you, so focused on wearing your mask, there likely are people all around you who are also masking themselves.

There are many signs of hurting people, but due to our busy, self-focused lives, it is easy to miss the obvious. There's the woman in an abusive relationship who routinely covers the physical and emotional scars she received at the hands of her abuser. It's easy—they say—to call the police or leave, but nobody knows her true story. We all deal or respond individually to situations based on our experiences. And you're not the only one she fooled.

Maybe a young woman has just had an argument with the man her mother told her to leave alone. Now guess who's at the door? Her mother. Of course, she can't confirm the fact that her mother was right about this man being nothing but trouble. So she tells him to be quiet as she opens the door with a smile. She pretends to be fine by living a lie. *Momma told me to leave him alone, didn't she?* But she ignores that fact and lies, not only to you but herself as well.

There is the little girl at school who has learned to be quiet about not having anything to eat for two days other than what the school cafeteria has served during lunchtime. At such a young age, she thinks her mother will get into trouble if she utters the words, "I'm hungry." So as a young girl, she has learned how to protect her mother from school and law officials. Nonetheless, when she leaves school, she is still hungry. Nothing has changed.

The mother covers for the child. The wife covers for her cheating husband. The husband covers up affairs that the wife has had with friends. Divorced women mask their true feelings. Most people don't tell their secrets. In most cases, everybody already knows them anyway. The abused woman uses makeup to cover her physical bruises. The drug addict covers up their needle marks. The alcoholic uses a brown paper bag or flask to conceal their drinks and mouthwash to get rid of the odor. The fired worker heads out to work every day covering up their failure. The thief covers up his crime by fencing the goods. The struggling student covers up the bad grades as long as she can until they are revealed.

What a difference a question like, "I'm going through A, B and C, can you help me?" can make when directed to the right person.

People all over the world, no matter what nationality or economic status, have masked or tried to cover up the shame of their pasts. They put on faces at home, work, school, social events, and yes, even at church. There are as many bandages and cover-ups as there are types of people. People are dying for help, crying on the inside, but they won't open their mouths and ask for help. I've seen it from the pulpit and while sitting in the pews. Let's take a peek into the lives of a few churchgoers, Mr. & Mrs. D.L and Mr. Do-Good.

MR. & MRS. D. L.

What a beautiful couple, the perfect image of love. They have the perfect son and daughter to complete the perfect family. This couple lives the good life. They are accustomed to the very best life has to offer. You go home comparing yourself and your spouse to these people because to you, they have it going on. They give you such a good feeling about their lives.

One Sunday, church is coming to a close, and you decide to beat the line to the ladies' room. You hear the church gossip telling another sister about the D.L.'s. You can't believe what you are hearing. He's what? Gay! You almost wet your underwear from the shock and then find yourself trying to lean in the direction of the voices on the other side of the stall's door. Is his affair with somebody in the church? To top it off, it's not him who is trying to keep everything hush-hush. It's the wife. She chooses to live with the lifestyle her husband has chosen. After all, no one can know she is married to a homosexual because what would people think?

MR. DO-GOOD

We will call him Mr. Do-Good. He seems like a true gentleman. He looks good and seems to cherish his wife. He operates his own business and works well at the church. There's not a Sunday that you haven't seen Mr. Do-Good at church. Each Sunday, he sits in the pews while the congregation believes all is well in his home. His wife and children look like the picture of perfection. In fact, you wish your family was just like them. That is until you find out by watching the six o'clock news that Mr. Do-Good is far from being a good man. He is arrested for beating his lovely wife and putting her in the hospital. Eventually, his wife testifies that she has endured this abuse repeatedly and finally told her secret because she was tired and wanted to stop masking her pain and covering up *his* sin.

What is the common denominator in these two scenarios? The hurting parties feared judgment. Not from God, but from people. They trembled at the possibility of those infamous yet deadly words, "What will people think?"

Masking is serious business, especially when we think we know a person's story. People will die covering up their sins if no one will help them. How can you help? Start by telling your story to offer aid to another soul. Yes, it's a sacrifice. But it just might save a life. Allow me to show you another example.

<u>BETHANY</u>

You are standing in the take-out line at McDonald's, and you make eye contact with the woman in front of you. Your eyes lock before you briefly look away. You make eye contact again. This time, she glances away. But something in her eyes captures your attention, even though you can't quite detect what is there. You don't think too much about it. After all, you're just waiting your turn in line.

The next day in the newspaper, you see a woman's picture. It's a photo of the same lady you saw in the line at McDonald's yesterday. Yes, the same woman. The caption reads, WOMAN FOUND DEAD IN BEDROOM.

You are rendered speechless. As you read the article, you learn the woman committed suicide. The woman in the line was masking. She was simply going through the motions of life not speaking a word, knowing she planned to end it all. She was doing what she knew to do, a familiar way of operating to get through the day. Did she tell anyone she was depressed? What if she did tell somebody that she felt like giving up, and they didn't listen? What if she cried and no one heard her?

In death, someone will hear her story and know that she cried, although it won't help her now. The woman is gone, never to breathe again.

In this scenario, I believe the woman was boxed in by her circumstances. There were choices in her life that scarred her. People may have hurt this woman and there were probably things she had done that she wanted to keep private. Even so, what would make someone willingly leave his or her children, or husband or wife? What was so bad about his or her life that it deserved a death sentence? Don't judge. Everybody handles obstacles differently. I remember this place all too well.

These are the effects of remaining quiet and trying to deal with matters alone. We must be careful how we deal with folks because we don't know what's going on in their lives. It's no secret some people tend to try to be more than who they are. Others walk around with the mindset that they are the lowest of the low on earth.

Who will dare stand up and tell the naked truth? With no one to bare her soul to, Bethany took matters into her hands. What would have happened if Bethany had found one person to talk to about her problems or maybe one person who would have loved her, gave her a hug or a smile? What if someone shared their testimony such that Bethany discovered she wasn't alone and that it was possible to overcome her problems?

There are many Bethanys in this world. I was one. Nobody knew my story, but many thought they did. I know because they tried to tell me how I should be. They took a sentence or two from my life's story and tried to write my entire book. They only had a page, at most, yet they used it to talk against me because they didn't understand my struggles.

Silence can kill. If there's no safe ear, what will happen to all those around us who are hurting? Where will they find hope? Who will tell them there's a better way than masking?

God has the beat of your life's drum. He knows what makes each of us thrive and that which causes us to faint. He knows just how much we can bear. This is because God has more than a page of our lives. He has the *entire* book. As we look at these people in the next few pages, we will clearly see how our conclusions are not what matters. Regardless of how long and the reasons why these individuals may have lived in silence, our focus should be on offering the love that can make all the difference.

UNMASK:

- What incidents in your life have prompted you to hide your true face?
- How often have you hid your true feelings behind a smile?
- What led you to do this? Be real.
- What does unmasking mean to you?

Chapter Eight
SILENCE IS NOT THE ANSWER

T o have knowledge of one rumor, paragraph, page, or chapter of somebody's life doesn't mean you know their entire story. We have all been guilty of drawing conclusions about people without knowing them. Having a few facts about a person doesn't mean we know them. We don't want others to judge us for our sinful acts; therefore we need to be careful about identifying and judging sin in the lives of others.

When I struggled with my past, I would have my story on the tip of my tongue, ready to share with Lucy, but a few seconds later, Lucy would talk about another sister in Christ. *Nope. She is not the person I need to trust with this secret.* Even then, I knew to guard my pain and my secrets. I could only share my heart with people I trusted. And for me, trust didn't come easy. I cared too much about how people thought of me to take a chance and share my heart with a gossip. Lucy attended church with me, but she wasn't trustworthy. Because of this, I remained silent.

Have you ever gone to church and felt like you couldn't let anyone see you cry? I remember all too well how people reacted when a couple of tears fell from my eyes. The women would congregate around me to ask questions, some sincere and some just nosey. "What's wrong? What happened?"

I didn't know who to trust. So, I said nothing. They could study what they already knew about me and draw their conclusions. Those women weren't seeking to help. They were seeking to know. I understand why people make the decision not to share. Unfortunately, too many times, they were right to wish they hadn't discussed their personal issues. Have you ever shared something and wished later you had kept your mouth closed because your business was in the streets or on Facebook? Some people lend their ear only to be a mouthpiece for judgment and gossip. Ask God to lead you to the right person to confide in. A God-given confidant will open their mouth in prayer and intercede for you.

DON'T FORGET WHERE YOU CAME FROM!

What would you do if someone came to you and shared all their precious life history? You listen. You even see yourself in their story.

What if you heard Linda share her story about how she was going to move in with Tyrone? And in sharing the detail of this plan, she admits her ultimate goal is to see if they are compatible in bed.

Of course, she wants to know other things. But, his bedroom skills are at the very top of the list. You know from experience this would be a terrible move for her. She's setting herself up for failure. She would be compromising a lot to get that coveted engagement ring. You know this firsthand because you lived it. You moved in with your Tyrone, and three kids later, you are still living together, but not married.

You can't help but remember the struggles you and the love of your life went through. Yet, you remain silent. Instead of telling Ms. Linda what you endured and what you learned in the process, you only say, "I'll pray for you." Why remain silent?

Never pass up an opportunity to share your testimony and experience. Your trials, tribulations, and triumphs can help others. If you are discerning, you can take your story and help another woman avoid unnecessary heartache. It takes courage and vulnerability to testify the truth to her. God helped you through it so you can help someone else avoid it.

I understand you don't want anybody to know about your situation, especially that this man who said he loved you didn't marry you after all. You thought things would turn out differently for you. In fact, you're still waiting for the Lord to help you with this one. If you say nothing, your silence is a form of agreement with Ms. Linda's choices. You're giving her the nod and, ultimately, inviting her into the same heartbreak you face.

It would be okay to say, "Girl, don't do it! I messed up when I did the same thing."

You tell yourself that you don't want to be in someone else's business. But you're already in her business. She told you.

Don't allow fear cloaked as courtesy to silence you. Maybe she's telling you her drama, so you'll help her say no and do the right thing. You already know—and she needs to hear—that moving ahead of God only sentences us to endure potentially painful circumstances as the consequence of our actions.

A few weeks later, you find out this young lady, the one you could have helped, the one who pulled you aside one Sunday, is no longer attending church. You haven't seen or heard from her. There's no way to reach her because her phone is now disconnected. The last resort is to stop by her place unannounced, and you do so only to find her apartment vacant. Now, what can you do? If only you had shared your past to help her avoid the same path you walked.

God used my son to pick me up off the living room floor. If he can use a child to save my life, he can use you to speak life and correction into your friends. Always do it with love.

Have you ever felt the urge to share personal bits of your past with others? That may be the Holy Spirit nudging you to help someone in their time of need. Help doesn't always mean writing a check. Sometimes it means baring your soul. Don't allow pride to hold you back.

I believe people are in a place where they need to hear the testimony of the deliverance of others. Your life could be the catalyst to encourage others to press forward. Sure, it can be embarrassing sharing about relationships, car repossessions, home foreclosures, abuse, or whatever the case may be. It was hard for me. But, I told my story. I survived and explained how God brought me out. My past is only a season of my life. It is not who I am. Neither is yours.

How quickly we forget that we haven't always been holy. Even after becoming holy, we still mess up. I agree that everyone doesn't need to know about our old struggles or habits. Being connected to God will help you discern when to share and when to keep quiet. Everybody has something God needs to clean up.

What would happen if people found out about your past? I had to come to the place where it didn't matter. Getting there has been a process in my life. What good does it do to selfishly protect or hide past mistakes and pain when my testimony might help save someone's life? You will know when it's the right time to share your testimony. The pain of others will compel you to open your mouth. You may not have to give all the intimate details, but bits and pieces could certainly make a difference. You could save a life. Telling my story saved a family member's life. Her mother was contemplating an abortion, and I told my story. With tears, she changed her mind and didn't go to the clinic. Her child is here today because I shared my mistake—my story.

DELIVER THE NEXT SISTER OR BROTHER

Your journey serves two purposes: to draw you closer to God and to show the love of God to others (1 Peter 1:22).

102

What you endured helped make you who you are. And, when you look back over your life you will see that others spoke life into you. They said or did something to help you push through your pain. Your circumstance is bigger than you but smaller than God. He uses all of it to show us how to serve one another.

An unmasked person is more powerful than a masked person. One operates in truth; the other operates in lies. God created us with a need to live and to know that truth (Psalm 51:6).

Bethany went to church with her cup in her hand, looking for a drink, only to be left drinking from the fountain of death. How did I make it and Bethany didn't?

Everything I did, all the seasons I conquered is because of Christ. I've been redeemed, and it's all under the blood now. That's why I have no problem being real. The mask is off. I am in a new place, ready to help a sister or brother up from the low places in life. Helping others come up is my heartbeat and passion in all that I do. I can finally show my scars from life. I have become a sister who is not afraid to bleed, allowing my scar tissue to show so healing can come to others. It's time out for kicking someone when they are down. Tell your story of how it was then and how it is now. You overcame (Revelation 12:11). Break the silence.

Telling only half the truth is still a lie. Layers and layers of untruths cover all the mess in the lives of people you see every day. Silence is a powerful façade. In my case, it was wrong for me to remain quiet. Not only did it prolong my healing process, it also crippled my ability to help others. Had I broken the silence, my freedom would have arrived sooner.

When you cover up your issues and keep secrets, it can cause permanent damage and leave people to be lost (Proverbs 28:13). The person covering up their issues will eventually cry out, "I do need help! I can't take this any longer!" This is precisely what happened to me.

SILENCE WAS THE GLUE THAT HELD MY MASK TOGETHER

When I decided to tell my secrets, I had a few false starts. But I kept going and soon realized not everyone would get the *unveiled* me. I had to remember how someone else responded to their abuse or incidents was not *my* story. When the same act happens to three different people, three different outcomes surface. As a result of our differences—personality, upbringing, and surrounding circumstances—our experiences yield different results. Remember, God made each of us fearfully and wonderfully. We are all different, and for people to insinuate somebody else's situation wasn't "that bad" is poor judgment. No one has the right to downplay you. It's *your* walk.

Don't be discouraged by the negativity that comes from people you thought were in your corner. They didn't know the real you before you removed your mask and may not be what you need for complete deliverance. God will send the divine connections you need for your safe and sacred place of healing. Keep going.

As I said, I stumbled a few times before I began to share. My "oath of silence" started breaking piece by piece. A few times I shared with the wrong people. Other times I shared with the right people at the wrong time.

My sister fell into the *right person at the wrong time* category. Granted, she knew about the abuse but didn't know the gory details. My sister is a protector and became agitated and angry when I brought up the abuse. I now know that she harbored her own guilt for not being able to do something to protect me. I quickly learned the thought of my abuse could make her snap. I left it alone because she wasn't ready.

Then I tried the most logical person in my mind, a male friend at the time. I tested the waters by telling him only the basics, but he lost it and verbally attacked my mother who, until then, had no idea the depth of what her daughter had encountered. Surely, he was the wrong person.

That was not the way I wanted my mother to find out. Huge mistake! I felt her pain as she became quiet after our conversation. The reveal was done all wrong, and I didn't like how he blamed my mother. She was *not* the problem. The person who abused me was. Unfortunately, not telling my mother made her a victim as well. That was a hard dose of reality. Telling an outsider before I told my mother caused her unnecessary pain. My mother didn't want to know that her child was not "handled with care."

After that failed attempt, I shut down. But, it wouldn't take long before I opened up again. God had already set up a place—a safe place—for me to release all of it. The words came easily with Tony, and I was able to tell him within a couple of months of meeting him. I told him everything—even how I behaved *to make them pay* as I got older.

As the words flowed, I felt embarrassed and empowered at the same time. The guilt and turmoil haunted me as I spoke of the incidents. I couldn't believe I was saying these things aloud where someone other than myself could hear. I cried and laughed at some of my creative ways of bringing this buried filth to light. Tony held me as needed when I wasn't animated. Even though he didn't allow me to confirm it, I felt him flinch a few times as he embraced me, while I recounted things.

Imagine the weight of my story on the shoulders of the man I had just started dating. He fought his inner battle with anger because he couldn't wrap his brain around someone treating a child that way. A child that had grown into the woman he fell in love with. He handled it because he is a protector and a stable and loyal friend.

UNMASK:

- How did this chapter offer insight into how people mask?
- What in this chapter challenged you?

- In what way did you see yourself in the pages of this chapter?

Chapter Nine
CAN I TELL YOU MY STORY?

❧

"Can I talk to you for a minute?"

That question is often the kiss of death or the beginning of an argument for romantic relationships. Even in platonic relationships, those words often give us pause, causing us to put up our guard.

What if those words came from a friend seeking someone to trust with the secrets of their hearts? What if those words came from someone who needed the balm of a friendship rooted and grounded in the love of Christ?

Could you be trusted with delicate information? Would you throw up a wall or accept the information only to make it gossip, thriving off someone else's trouble? If you want to be used by God, you must decide to be a trustworthy person and safe place for ministry. We are all called to fulfill The Great Commission by making disciples of the nations (Matthew 28:9). Jesus led the first disciples. He taught them. He listened to them. He loved them. He gave them something tangible and real to believe in. Could you do this for others?

Remember, people mask their truths because of the fear of judgment, ridicule, and rejection. They know many of us can't handle the truth about our own lives let alone the pain and suffering of others. There are few people who are naturally capable of listening without judgment. However, this skill can be learned and developed. It all begins with a choice to treat others as you want them to treat you (Matthew 7:2; Luke 6:31).

If someone came and told you they were struggling with lust, pornography, lying, stealing, or homosexuality, what would you say? How would you address the problem that was presented in confidence? The person who confides in you does so because you share core values and beliefs. They *trust* you. For them, the struggle comes from knowing they are living in conflict with their convictions.

Confession of our faults is biblical and brave. Are you brave enough to battle alongside your sister or brother in Christ? Or, would you take the coward's way out and align with the enemy by accepting personal and confidential information, and then sharing it with others in gossip? Would you force the person who is hurting to remain quiet in fear of that type of rejection?

When you breach the trust of a person who confides in you, you cause them to retreat and believe that no one can know. *I can't tell a soul* are the words that will haunt them as you laugh at and gossip about them.

Listening to help someone is a great task. There were times I opened up and received the right religious jargon, but it was laced with the wrong spirit. That is hurtful not helpful. A pure heart or spirit will love the person right where they are.

Be the help you needed when you were going through something. Remember how it felt to be so weary that you could only see your problem and not God.

If you're still going through a situation, ask God to place the right people on your path—people who can help you overcome your test so you can share your testimony. Remember there is nothing too big for God to heal and no sin too awful for Him to forgive.

<u>AT CHURCH</u>

Remember Bethany, the young woman from McDonald's who committed suicide in Chapter Seven? Let's look at the last days of her journey.

After much contemplation, pain, and rejection, Bethany decided to walk to church to see if she could learn about this God she'd heard about. Upon arrival, Bethany saw groups of adult churchgoers walking into the building, dressed to the nines, in starched-pressed suits, professionally shined shoes, and beautiful dresses with matching hats. Even the children's attire was meticulously chosen. Having heard the much-used sentiment 'come as you are,' the young woman felt grossly underdressed in her worn jeans and faded t-shirt.

Her first thought was to turn around and go home. She had misunderstood that coming to church with what she had on the night before was okay. But her curiosity made her stay *to see* what happens. Bethany had already made up her mind to end it all if this didn't work.

"Hello, how are you?" a young lady with a bright smile and welcoming eyes greeted Bethany as she stood at the doors of the church. "Welcome to our church."

The warmth emanating from the young woman confirmed Bethany's decision to stay. It had been a while since someone had spoken to her with kindness. If she were honest, Bethany had to admit that few people over the past few months had even noticed her. Even at church, most people walked right by her without a *hello* after their glances.

Still a little embarrassed about her attire, Bethany tried to slide into a pew near the back of the church, but a man with white-gloved hands directed her to the middle of the church. A woman with white-gloved hands showed her a seat on the end of the row. *This makes for an easy exit* Bethany thought as she took her seat. She observed the people around her.

Some people worshiped with their hands raised high. Others danced with the same fervor as local nightclub patrons. Occasionally, she'd see a young woman touch up her lip-gloss.

There were a few people who, like her, simply sat and watched, taking it all in but not participating.

The people at church appeared as though they had it all together. Bethany, however, felt small and needy, like she didn't belong. *Why did the others come if they were fine?* Bethany noticed something eerily familiar about some of the faces in the congregation. She saw the deception and knew what it was. They were wearing something Bethany had on herself—masks.

They had their game faces on, but they needed help just like she did. Any good player who knows the game can spot other players on the team. This was not the place Bethany wanted to be if it meant covering things up. She could do that without the help of a congregation. She was already doing it. Bethany was not at peace with her mask any longer, so she left.

The masked congregants drove her away. She came to church looking for something different than what she had. She hoped to find people who had figured out *how* to be authentic, how to be real. Instead, she found mirror images of herself—the persona she wanted to escape. She needed to feel the love that would push her away from the old familiar, desperate place and bring her into a new one. She wanted to enter a place of hope and acceptance. Bethany wanted freedom, rest from pain. Worshipping in the presence of God with no cover-up might have helped the healing process begin. After all, the church was supposed to be for the sick and the brokenhearted.

112

When all you see are "perfect people" who cover up real issues with designer suits, shoes, and the best hairdos, it is hard to see yourself fitting in with other worshippers. Please don't get me wrong. Dressing nice is great, but a well-adorned and pristine outer appearance does little to mend the brokenness inside. Bethany left church feeling the same way she did when she arrived—lost, broken, and alone. The strand of rope she held on to unraveled.

The church of the living God is the place you and I should both be able to go to (1 Timothy 3:14-16). Praying men and women of God should be there to greet you and to meet your needs through discernment, not assumption. It shouldn't matter if you dress like a supermodel or a beggar, someone should see your needs and help you. If only Bethany could have run to the Lord instead of running out of the church. If only the people present in the church had removed their masks, they would have seen her pain because they would have been open to it. Masks impede your vision.

How many men and women like Bethany have walked away from us, hurt or misguided? What have we become? Have we forgotten our trying times? Our hurt? Our pain? What if we could tap into the "Bethany's" around us? What if we felt their hearts and prayed for them? We have gotten so busy that we don't even wait for the response of others. We pay little, if any, attention to the signs before us. People in mental, emotional, and spiritual pain steadily drift away while we fail to toss them the life-preserving power of the Holy Spirit. It's time to allow our hearts to lead us, not our clocks.

I DIDN'T SEE HER MASK

I had a friend who joyfully left church one Sunday. In fact, she was an encouragement to me that day. The next day I learned she had written letters to her family and friends to say *goodbye*. As she laughed with and encouraged me, she had already decided that life was too much. She was giving me the very best her masked life could offer. And, I received.

It made me think of all the times I had served others while I was in pain. I changed diapers as my soul ached. I went to work as my soul ached. I showed up at church as my soul ached. I'm sure I even tried to speak life into others the Sunday before I decided to take my life. I understood her pain because I had been there. I had smiled, pretending that everything was okay while preparing to end it all.

I knew she was hiding something, but she kept telling me she was all right. I took her word for it and didn't bother to call, pray for, or check on her. Even though I couldn't put my finger on it, I felt there was something different. Thankfully, we serve and all-knowing, all-seeing, and caring Father. He showed up in the nick of time, and that young woman is still in the land of the living.

I might not have been praying fervently for her, but someone was. Someone saw through the façade. When you've mastered wearing a mask, it takes the Master to uncover you.

God wants you to live whole and free, so He sends help by placing you on the hearts of others. Sometimes they pray for you. Other times, they will offer kind words or simply a knowing squeeze of the hand. Some will deliver an encouraging message. *This too shall pass.* Then some people will come right out and ask if everything is okay or if you need to talk.

Don't reject help when you're in need. If you're afraid, ask God to give you discernment on whom to go to for help. If you don't get help, your problems will keep a death grip on your throat and drain you of life. It will cause you to reach for things that will pacify the situation and not bring the true healing that is needed. The new day begins when we admit that everything isn't quite all right (Hebrews 5:14).

SOME CALL THE DOCTOR

Bethany tried going to a stranger, a psychiatrist, because she thought it would be easier. There were no strings attached, and they couldn't legally reveal her problems to others. I understand that God uses doctors, but in this case, Bethany used the prescribed medication to avoid the problem. She already couldn't think straight, and the pills just put her in a barely functional daze. Her sense of reality would come and go as she abused the pills to numb the emotional pain. The medication didn't work because it couldn't reach the problem at its core. There's only One who can uproot the seed of destruction. She called the wrong doctor (Matthew 4:23).

FAMILY

In Bethany's life, she was always the one people came to with their problems. She felt because they depended on her to be strong, she couldn't "burden" them with her weakness. Her mind couldn't fathom telling her story to people she helped. She kept quiet about her sins and problems, and the price she paid was her very own life. Silence is never the answer.

As previously stated, no one wants to tell their problems to people with loose lips. All of us have that friend or family member who can't help but share "juicy gossip." The key is identifying the ones who can handle you becoming undressed before them. You watch, you listen to their conversations, and over time you can discern if you've found your safe person. The downfall is some family members won't forget and may remind you of your confession as soon as the opportunity arises. It helps to extend your definition of family to people who are faith-related, but not necessarily blood-related when seeking help (Proverbs 27:10).

A family is comprised of people, whether biological or not, who provide a place of peace and security where you feel at home. There's always somebody, maybe even someone you least expect, who will listen and hear you. This will allow you to begin your process of healing as you take off the mask.

THIS IS IT—I LET GO!

After we have tried everything else, we will all eventually go down to our knees, kneeling at the Master's feet. We've held on to "it" long enough. It's time. He's the perfect One to go to because He's the One who made you and me. When you go to Him, you will find that He's been waiting for you all along. As you and I go back and forth, trying this and that, God is saying, "Here I am."

When my moment came, I thought, *I should have done this a long time ago*. I went through a lot of unnecessary turmoil instead of allowing God, who made me, fix my brokenness and put me back together as a whole person.

How did I do it? I broke open before Him. I opened my mouth and shared and shared until I couldn't share anymore. As things came to mind, I told God about my hurts. I confessed everything (1 John 1:9). Letting go made me feel clean. The things suppressed for years came up from deep within my gut and spilled out of my mouth. There's nothing like your prayer reaching God's ears (1 Peter 5:6). I told God every detail of my pain and asked Him to free me from masking my past to cover my shame. This book is proof He answered my prayer.

What happened after that? He still loved me even after I told him the gut-wrenching truth. Even knowing all of my mess, He loved me still.

Like a gentleman, God waited for me to come to Him and open up my heart. I was precious to Him, the apple of His eye (Psalm 17:8).

He loves you the same way. There is no love or feelings of wholeness you can receive from anyone other than our Heavenly Father. For God so loved (insert your name) that He gave His one and only Son that (insert your name) who believes in Him shall not perish but have eternal life (John 3:16). You have to receive His love for you. You have to believe He loves you because He does. Your relationship with Him is personal.

When I knew without a doubt that God loved me, I put my past in His hands. Everything that made me hide behind a mask of otherness, I gave to Him. I gave my troubles to the One who can handle all things, and I didn't take them back (1 Peter 5:7).

Each time a problem or feeling came to me, I gave it to Him. I would say, "Lord, I don't like this feeling. I ask you to take it away and replace it with your love."

He answered me by offering me His love until the thing that haunted me was no longer an issue. I remembered that God loved me. I did this with each painful situation. Small or huge, I sought God in every problem. Why? Because I am His child, I can go to Him. He gave me the privilege to come before Him with all things. He directed my steps and helped me stay on the right path. He brought deliverance while I was sprawled out on my living room floor.

Do I ever get off track? Yes. But, I always find that I will come back to God. He knows the way I should go. His Word says my steps are ordered by Him (Psalm 37:23, Psalm 119:105).

Letting go of your problems requires total trust in God and a heart that is willing to admit you need Him. And, you need loving people to support you. You must trust in God's ability to orchestrate your life.

While God blesses us with abilities, it is His provision and favor that blesses us. In other words, you can't out do God. You can't outwork God. You need Him. To be in His will, you must let go of the reins. It worked for me. It will work for you.

I am His child. You are His child. This eternal relationship began the day we gave our lives to the Lord, by accepting Jesus Christ as our Lord and Savior. This relationship gives us access to Him—the almighty, all-knowing, powerful God—in prayer (Hebrews 4:16).

God will send folks to build you up and encourage you, but your rock, your solace, and your endurance should always be in Him. It's better to reach for God first to avoid all the drama. He is the One to go to, and He patiently waits for us to recognize that and respond.

He is everything. I now trust Him to take care of me. In doing so, I have become a safe place for the people that I direct back to God. He doesn't want us hiding behind masks. God wants us liberated as we accept His love.

He sees and knows you anyway because He holds every detail of the story. He's seen every page, and He still loves you and me the same (1 Peter 4:8).

UNMASK:

- How did this chapter affect you?

- Are you a safe place for someone to land?
- How would you handle a conversation with someone who wanted to unmask before you?

Chapter Ten
DON'T LET THE DEVIL NAME YOU!

❦

Say your name.

No, really. I mean it. Say your name right now. Out loud.

How does it sound to you?

If you didn't say it, go on and do it.

How does it sound to you?

There's no sound like the name that has been given to you. This is the name people call you and the one you answer to. You must know your name; otherwise, you'll respond to anything.

Pain, rejection, and fear will attempt to wrap around you. Instead of answering to the name your parents gave you, you will start to answer to the names the world calls you. Your past or temptation can call your name because it knows you will listen. If you don't know your name, you'll answer to something that can take hold of you and tear you down. That something will try to call you

121

its own. To resist this pull, you need to know the sound of your name.

Have you ever been in a crowded room and someone you didn't know called your name? Let's say your name is Susan. A stranger walks into the room and says, "Susan." There are two Susans. You don't move, but the other Susan does. The person that called *her* name is her husband. You didn't move because you didn't recognize the voice. Simply put, the call was intended only for her.

My name represents my parents' bloodline, their history, and my purpose journey. What's greater than all of that is the blood of Jesus that calls me. I respond to that call because that's who I am. But I didn't always answer. Sometimes I was too busy allowing my situation to give me a name. Tired. Depressed. Suicidal. Mask Wearer. Fornicator. Liar.

Those were my names until I responded to Jesus. That's when He called me to my purpose. Blessed. Child of God. Daughter of the King. An Heir to the Kingdom. Writer. Prayer Warrior.

Did you notice the difference in what God calls me versus what sin calls me? Who are you answering to? What sin keeps calling your name trying to destroy you?

Suicide made daily calls to me. Initially, I just let the thoughts visit. I didn't immediately say *it's time to end it* all. My actions acknowledged that I believed that was my name. At the time, I didn't know the true essence of my name. But when I found out I was answering the wrong calls, I began to listen to my name and the voice of the caller. I soon stopped answering to every call of distress, temptation, and discouragement from my enemy. It just didn't sound right anymore. I learned to tune into the Shepherd's voice.

I wasn't named to respond to molestation, abuse, and emotional turmoil. I wasn't named to respond to sin. My name stands for something greater, something good. Thank God I stopped answering the devil's calls. As I listened, God began to make the sound clear for me to hear, and I could tune into the things that meant me good. In the process of retraining my ear, He cleansed me of things I once allowed to control my life.

Those things couldn't call and get an answer anymore because I began to only respond to the voice of my Father.

NAMES DO HURT YOU

Some of us have been called out of our given name so often we have started to believe our name has changed. Acting out of a false name is detrimental to our spiritual and emotional well being. Whether you have been called stupid, loser, tramp, jailbird, homosexual, prostitute, no-good, liar, worthless—whatever the slur—remember this: It is not your name!

Those names are stumbling blocks to your spiritual growth. They are meant to call you to a place of darkness and tear down your faith. These names and sinful acts once summoned you by the power of seduction from the pit of hell. You were enticed by the sinful desires that dwelled in your wicked heart. You attract what you secretly meditate on.

It's true. I've been there. That sin responded to what was attached to you or what you are putting out there. Sin will look for a home to abide. Then the sin is recycled in your life, and you still find yourself unfulfilled despite believing the lies, because "it" or "they" can't fulfill you. Only the One who knows your name can fulfill you.

When we respond to lies, it causes us to drift farther away from who we were created to be. Our behavior traps us to the point of living in sin, ashamed for anyone to know what we've thought about or what we have done. Then, we put on masks.

Instead of facing our sin, we hide, giving into sin's seduction. Giving in takes a part of you. It takes your name. It strips you of who you are.

I say it takes our name because when we come to ourselves, it takes a while for us to rid ourselves of yesterday and receive a renewed mind. If you've asked God for forgiveness, you may still have to go through some trials to free yourself. Some of us beat ourselves up or spend the rest of our lives trying to make up for what we have done even though we have been forgiven.

Too often, we answer temptation's call because it knows our name. We know the sound of sin. We've been set up before to fail. Sometimes we—ourselves—light the candles and set the mood. Whatever your "thing" is can trap you and pull you away from what God named you. As your "thing" names you, it no longer has to seduce you. Your name has been changed. Instead of your "thing" searching for you, you search for your "thing."

When the enemy steals your name, your identity soon follows. You lose yourself. You can't seem to separate yourself from the sin. You see yourself as something other, and you become it. You try to hide your sin behind masks, but eventually, everyone will see your secrets. Sin has a unique scent. The Bible says your sin will find you out. It's true.

Captions and headlines all over the world start with these words: MAN KILLS WIFE and CHILDREN...WOMAN CAUGHT ON TAPE...EMPLOYEE EMBEZZLES THOUSANDS...WIFE FOUND DEAD IN ANOTHER MAN'S BED...

Don't let your sin lead you to a place of defeat. Deal with it. The devil, your enemy, is the opposite of God. Whatever dwells in the darkness is an enemy of God. Therefore, evil is our enemy, too.

Anything that comes to steal life from you does not have your best interests at heart. The things we try to hide, our "undercover" sins, will allow the enemy to keep sin and fear of being caught over our heads.

The enemy sets up camp until you drive him out. You must let it be known that sin, the devil, and his imps are no longer welcome. You must tell the enemy to leave.

Silence is not golden when you can open your mouth and kick out your tormenter. Remaining silent is a passive aggressive way to go along with an enemy who intends to destroy you. Tell the devil to take a hike in Jesus' name.

Life has tried to name you "down and out." Perhaps, it has uttered you will never be free. But, God said it is well. When the world gives up on you, God has the last word, and He will never leave you or forsake you (Hebrews 13:5). Life happens, but you have to keep on going, keep on dealing with each bump as it comes your way. God is with you.

Some men and women have successful businesses and degrees, but they still respond to names that don't belong to them. People in every walk of life have problems and mask their existence. The devil wants to destroy everyone he can. He doesn't care how much money or education you have. He doesn't care where you live. He just wants you eliminated.

He does this by changing your name and making you believe you are not worthy of God's love and help. He wants you off-course from your purpose. It's a sidetrack to call you his own. Know your name.

DON'T ANSWER THE CALL

Let's look at the young lady who is so beautiful and successful that no one would think there's anything wrong with her. By all accounts, it appears she has a perfect life. But she battles loneliness. She's been waiting for the right man, and frankly, she's tired of this unanswered prayer. The enemy sees this and assigns her a new name: DESPERATION.

Her desire for a mate grows until she is desperate to find one. The enemy grows excited at her weakness and waits for an opportunity to get beneath her skin. She begins to compromise by lowering her standards and not waiting for a godly man.

Next thing you know, Johnny Slick Rick comes along. Normally, Johnny wouldn't get the time of day, but she wants, no needs, a man to combat the loneliness. He takes her for the ride of her life. And, it's a costly ride. She loses everything she's worked hard to attain.

Instead of enjoying her success, she meditated on her loneliness until she couldn't take it anymore. She decided to find a man instead of wait for a husband. The devil called her *lonely,* and then he called her *desperate.* He didn't call her beautiful or successful. She listened to the devil's taunts when he called her an *old maid.* Eventually, she got a man who abandons her, because he shouldn't have been in her life. He was a distraction. The young lady is alone, again. Only this time, she's worse off than she was before.

The enemy can name you or target a weakness. It is up to you to let him in or send him away. Maybe you struggle with lust, and you can't shake thoughts of an attractive coworker. The thoughts are sexual in nature, and they build over time the more you dwell on them. You think *what would it be like to share a night of passion with them*? Or you wonder if they'd do this or that with you. Even though you have a spouse who does all those same things in the bedroom, this person who is not your spouse captivates you, and your curiosity is piqued to the point of distraction. Your mind is out there, working against you and your name. While you are in the midst of fantasizing, the enemy is naming you—"Adulterer." He's changing your name to whet your appetite until you become what you are obsessing over. While you think these are harmless thoughts that aren't hurting anyone, he's chuckling and saying, "Gotcha!"

Homosexuality starts with thoughts until the enemy comes to make them a reality. As with anything else, sin begins in the mind. When we ponder and meditate on the wrong things, they consume us. We become those things. We lose our identity.

There is another option. Meditate on the things of God. Change your mind—it will change your life. Every idea starts with a thought. When we disciple our thoughts, it makes us aware of when the enemy attacks. This is why we must hold every thought captive.

You need to believe unbridled thinking will lead to nowhere but trouble. How can it not? The Word of God says, "As a man thinks...so he is" (Proverbs 23:7).

You must scream, "That's not my name! You are calling me by the name of something I was only a participant in. It's not me."

The accuser will remind you of everything you've ever done and try to take you back into captivity. He wants your name to be a part of his story. He wants you to self-destruct. We have to leave these places of slavery for good. We must separate ourselves from people, places, and things that will take us back to living a lie. The devil wants to name us for all eternity. Listen to God's voice, and live in the truth.

Your name is priceless. There's no one in the world exactly like you. God knows who you are, and that's worth more than life itself. He called my name in my darkest hour, and I responded because, through the noise, I heard my name. I knew my name. I rose up to finally say, "Enough!"

Even in sin, we will hear God and feel the nudge in our spirits because He made us in His image. We can sense Him there. Even people who have never called on God before will call His name on the brink of a car accident or a plane crash. As they say, there are no atheists in foxholes. Simply put, it's in us to call Him God.

Suicide kept calling me, saying my name. It tried to come at me in a new way, but with God's help, I could sense or discern what was going on. When you are no longer hiding behind the things you used to do, you come to a new name. Expose sin in prayer.

Lord, I'm tempted by (say the name, call it out, break the power). Please forgive me. I close the door to this temptation in the name of Jesus. Help me to stand. In the name of Jesus. Amen.

Call things that tempt you what they are—temptation. Don't let them name you. Don't let your sin name you. God has your name and a sound just for you. But you must position yourself to listen to

His voice. Stop recalling past failures, the words of naysayers, and the pain of rejection and hear God's voice (John 10:4).

You will know when you hear your true name. You will begin to ignore calls from your enemies. You will begin to ignore nagging thoughts about past masks. You will no longer be tempted to call them back. In fact, the calls will no longer get through to you. You will find yourself saying, "I used to do that?" You won't believe you were once there because you will see how far you have come. You grow into a position to help someone else know their name.

The mask is off, baby, and I'll be the first person, to tell the truth. My name is Sonya, and I hear the sound of the Lord coming (Isaiah 62:2). Don't you hear Him?

The devil won't name me anymore. Please, don't let the devil name you.

UNMASK:

- It's not always negative words; sometimes it's the lack of humility. Pride will prevent us from admitting some things out loud. What names speak to you and how?

Chapter Eleven
WHO HAVE YOU BECOME?

R emember repeating the famous Jesse Jackson declaration "I am somebody" at school assemblies when you were a child? Everyone collectively chanted, "I am somebody!" With loud voices, we said those words to affirm our worth and value.

People pretend like they can do without the love. Or, they act as if they don't need it going through life wrapped in their sense of accomplishment. But, in their heart, love is exactly what they want. How many lies do folks tell when they are trying to be something other than who they are?

People need to feel loved and important. People of all races and cultures are searching for their true identities. In this, they seek validation through prestige and position to prove they are somebody.

My weakness became my identity crutch. I could no longer stand on the strength of a mask. I had to be introduced to the person I was. When your identity is covered behind a new face to adapt to the people you are with, or to a circumstance, you—the person—are no longer living. The mask lives and takes on a life of its own. You become who you emulate. You send a message that says, "This is all me." We often do this to escape ourselves. It is exhausting to put on a front and live a lie. It is so much better to be the true you, the authentic you, that you were created to be. There's a day coming when you will say, "I am who I am." The inward struggles and battles of measuring up in our strength will be over, and in your heart, you will know who you are. Until you choose to accept yourself, you will not live the truth, and the enemy of your soul will whisper back to you, "I know who you are when nobody's looking."

In preparation for this book, I created a survey. One of the questions asked was, "Who are you?" Many responded by telling me who their parents were; what they did for a living, their marital status, or where they lived. Most people didn't know how to respond to this question. We look for something to connect with, believing that will be our identity. But the question wasn't, "What do you do for a living?" or "Where do you live?" or "Who are your parents?" The unanswered question remains the same. "Who are you?" The real you…

OTHERS THINK THEY KNOW YOU

I've been at the grocery store or some other public place when someone who knows my family recognizes me. In each instance, they couldn't call my name. They reached for my mother's maiden name or my grandparents' names.

Instead of asking, "Baby, what's your name?" the stranger would stand there and try to tell me whose child I was by identifying my lineage. I have even tried to interrupt to speed up the process as my meat thawed and ice cream melted, but they wanted to guess. They'd say, "Don't tell me. I know ya!" Out of respect, I'd stand right there.

I'm sure this has happened to you as well. In my experience, people identify other people by their relatives, where they live, or where they work. Through association, they assume because they know your family, they know you. The next thing you know, they are hollering, "We kin." While that might be true, it still doesn't tell them my name.

Who we are is connected to our family roots at a foundational level. It's where your story begins here on earth, but it's not the totality of it. Who your family is is not a complete definition of who you are.

I am not my mother. I am her child. I am not the sister who was on the softball team. I am Sonya, the one who played the viola. I am not Jenny and 'em, Thelma, or Diane. I am me. The one who sat on the porch with a book in her hand because her mother told her to stay put. Yes, we are a branch of the family tree, but people still search for their reason for living. If my family roots were enough, I'd be complete with need of nothing else.

Have you ever had a teacher or a loved one ask you what you want to be when you grow up? I always answered this question with excitement, rambling off this and that. As I grew older, my career choices became more defined. I became those roles, working in administration and now as a writer. But my profession did not tell me who I was. It just said what I wanted to do to earn a paycheck.

Parents tell children and teenagers what they want them to be when they grow up. Some people are told they will never amount to anything. Both positive and negative voices take root in our lives, trying to point us in the direction others want us to become. All these ideas and voices are missing the mark. There's only One who knows the true story of who you are. He's the One who made you.

MANY ROLES, STILL NOT WHO I AM

Issues that I allowed to define me also defined how I lived and responded to life. From the day God used my son as a messenger, I became stronger because of the Lord. His hand reshaped me to be the person He created instead of who my circumstances made me become.

Everything we do in life requires a decision. Every choice we make affects our lives. As we mature and take on more responsibilities, our identities and the roles we play are ever evolving and expanding.

You can become a doctor, but who are you when you leave the hospital? You become a mother, but when you leave your child at the daycare and go to work, who are you?

We play so many roles because of the different hats we wear and the responsibilities we have in our lives. Those roles help shape an illusion. People relate to me out of the context of those role(s): wife, mother, daughter, sister, preacher, and writer. This means they know what I am doing at any given period during the day based on the role I'm functioning in when they encounter me. It does not mean they know who I am.

Many people would lose their identities if they lost their jobs. If their friends stopped calling and kicked them to the curb, they'd feel worthless. If their husbands walked away from the marriage, they'd feel used and abused, with no reason to live. Why? The job, the friends or the relationship is their ID card. Because of this wrong assumption of identity, when the job dissipates, the friends leave, and the husband walks out, they have no identity of their own for which to carry on.

People from all over the world feel that certain groups or connections can make them. Some believe if they had this job, this car, this house, this man or this woman, this many children, they'd have a perfect identity. If it were that simple, we'd all be okay. Things would be so much better because we've arrived and have achieved goals and received the thing or person that we desired. There would be no need to mask and no need to lie about who we are. Sadly, this is not the case. As we look at the stars in Hollywood

135

and the people we admire near and far, we see it takes more for us to be complete.

We cannot find our identities in people, places, or things. No matter how much or who we get, we will never be satisfied. Why? The missing link is the connection to our Creator. My identity, my reason for living, is not because of what I do, or who my friends are, but who I am by myself as I was created to be. If I don't know this, I live my life in vain.

Life happens to us daily. Each time we lie down and rise again, by the grace of God, we have to go on living whether we feel like it or not. It's strange because life still keeps going, and the days don't stop. You and I just take the things, goals, or problems from one day to the next. That is until something happens to cause us to be challenged in a new way of thinking and living.

People are stuck on what they do. When I punch the clock at work, I am an administrative assistant coordinator for five hours. When I leave, I am Sonya who has a variety of other roles to fulfill, and that's it. That job alone does not define who I am. It consists of tasks that I do.

Ask yourself, "Who am I when I take away all of the roles?" That's what I am talking about when I refer to the true you. It's that person. Sure, these roles are a part of us, but sometimes we can become lost in the daily motions of life. When I'm alone, who do I reveal? What face do I show? Why can't I show this person all the time? What's so bad about this person? Jesus knew this and preached on it many times. He is our example.

If you can answer the question of who you are with pure confidence, that's wonderful. I couldn't at one time. I had to find out about me and why God spared my life and not Bethany's. Why do I continue to exist?

YOU BECAME THE SIN

You become what you do. Whether good or bad, covered or revealed, you become what you say, think and do. Even through all the motions and roles, we are who we are. If I am playing a role, then I will not tell you who I am.

We can work side-by-side with someone for years, thinking we know them. We go to their weddings, celebrate the birth of their children, and add money to cards for their birthday. Sometimes we have dinner after work. Then, something major happens that breaks through the façade.

It might be a cheating or abusive spouse when we thought our coworker had the best marriage ever. Or, the coworker snaps and shoots up the workplace. Our surprise is a result of being tricked by the mask. Our coworkers do it and so do we.

Tragedy strikes when we don't deal with our issues. Sometimes it's difficult to figure out what's going on with the people we think we know. Even though you are with somebody, there are things you will never know about people until who they are underneath the mask surfaces, and it affects you in some manner.

137

Under all the politeness, smiles, and "I can help you" attitudes, they are a total wreck. They were probably this way all along. They hid behind masks, with those unchecked issues causing them to become the person they didn't want to be.

Let's say one day you picked up something that was not yours. Instead of it being a one-time lapse of good judgment, you continue to go around stealing, making this a habit. You have now become a thief. This is who you are because this is what you regularly do.

Now, let's say you messed around with a married person, leading to an act of adultery. Instead of asking God's forgiveness and determining not to do it again, you continue to tip into the same bedroom. You are now an adulterer. You are this thing because this is how you choose to live. Whether it turns into a permanent affair or not, because you are habitually violating your marriage vows, this is what you've become.

It's not a one or two-time mistake. Something has to be broken to stop you from such destructive behavior and thinking, or the pattern continues. If it's not with the same person, it will be with someone else. The seeds we sow, grow. Some issues obviously need to be dealt with if you continuously find yourself going down these bumpy roads. You say that it tells your story; it's what you do.

We say it's who we are by simply agreeing with the situations in our lives. It's what some have come to know about us. If this is the case and this is who you truly are, then why the secrets? The truth of the matter is if you keep going back to the drug or whatever your deal is, you will become the manifestation of the thing you do.

In other words, you can't continue to hide things and expect them to remain hidden. If you keep going back, you will become your deepest, darkest secret.

There are not any flags on the top of cars saying there goes a cheater, thief, or adulterer. We keep these things covered in our secret lives. It's what we have become in the dark that will find its way to the light. There are some who want to be free, but because this is what they've known, they say, "This *must be* who I am."

Don't quit in defeat because you can't see an exit. Jesus is the answer. He has the roadmap. He became sin for you to set you free.

WE'VE ALL DONE SOMETHING

There are those who never do anything wrong, at least in their minds. They always see everyone else's errors, but they don't see anything wrong with themselves. Ever take a good look at you? It's mirror-mirror time (1 Corinthians 4:5; Matthew 10:26).

Everybody has sinned or messed up somewhere in life. We may appear spotless and blameless because of the masks we wear. The Bible says in Romans 3:23, we have all fallen short of sinful acts, wrong attitudes, and superiority—those who think with "I'm better than you" personalities.

Our culture does a good job of painting a beautiful picture and showing all the pretty colors. Some muddy places run like a stream into the lives of people. It's time to become clean and naked before a Holy God. He knows all, sees all, and He's been there the entire time.

Sin invaded my life. Like you, it's only a part of my story. Thank God it doesn't have to be our benediction.

UNMASK:

- Who have you become?

- Take a few moments to think back to your childhood. What was your wildest dream? What did you want to be when you grew up?

- Now, consider this. Why did you want to be _____ when you grew up? I bet it had something to do with who God created you to be.

- Who or what is robbing you of the freedom to unveil who you are?

- What special skills and talents do you possess? In what way do you use them? Why or why not?

- Now, think about the dreams deferred as well as the ones you live. How did your circumstances shape your existence? How can you drop your mask and be the true you?

Chapter Twelve
WHO I AM

With a life surrounded by lies, I, in turn, became a lie, forgetting the truth most of the time. I wore a mask that allowed me to escape. Today, I am a real woman of God, who was introduced to Him before the storm. He got me through it, and He is keeping me safe now. When I began to know Him, I found out who I am.

No one can complete us except for the One who made us. God, my Creator, has the specs. My mother and father were the ordained vessels and watchmen over my life. I had to learn to live. My sisters and friends didn't make me Sonya. I had to figure out how to stand by myself. I got married, but my husband didn't make me complete because I still wasn't whole. These people influenced and helped shape my life, but it was God who gave me life. He *caused* me to live.

People will come and go, but you will always remain. In a crowded room, you hold your space. In a restaurant, you lift your hand to your mouth and feed yourself. Even in the hair salon or barbershop rotation system, the stylists work on one head of hair at a time. It's you. You matter. You make a difference. You stand alone until the good Lord says it's time to leave this place.

It's up to you whether you live behind a mask or choose to live uncovered. So far, we've had to deal with masking and not allowing silence to be the answer. Let's take off the mask and be real.

You can only do this by going to God, the one who made you. Prayerfully say, "Lord, here I am; show me the way." The masks will crack and eventually fall off. However, you must be willing to be broken to be made whole again. You must be willing to free yourself from the comfort of the mask. Living in freedom changes you because being free allows you to receive from the hand of the Father.

He told me who I was and now I know. I am not my own. I am His.

We talked about this some in previous chapters. God has the plans for you and will unveil them so you can find you. I didn't find out who I was until I found myself at the feet of Jesus. It was only then that I knew the truth. I came away from that experience humbly recognizing He's a great God. I am nothing without Him. God saw past all the messes I made in my life. In spite of all the dark places I held on to and all the incomplete places I needed Him to fill, He, God Almighty, wanted to do something with my life.

Of everything I could ever accomplish, it's what I do for the Lord that will remain. Hear me out. A job, people and things of this world will pass away. At the end of your career and your life, everything moves forward without you. Someone will fill the position at work. Your loved one will even learn how to live without you. But, the things of the Lord are eternal. Your life after this one is eternal.

I was a part of God's plan, but I first had to be real to receive it. I had to become naked before a Holy God. In other words, one by one, I took off each garment of death that plagued me. For so long, I had worn accessories to the garments of shame and guilt. I had to learn how to become free. I had lived in a covered state for so long that I had to find me. God knew me, but I had to come to my identity. The identity I have in Him.

THIS WAS MY BEGINNING

I was His child, born for a purpose—one of a healing ministry. That's who I am. It sounds wonderful, but there was a price I had to pay to get there. I had to sacrifice my life. I had to give up some things in my life and some people who were not good for me. I had to surrender myself to God and His ways. I had to take off the mask that I allowed the world to see and not be afraid to bleed in secret...or in public. Because of God, I can live free and not bound.

I never wanted to think about suicide again.

I had to get fitted for some better clothes, new garments. It was a job, let me tell you. I am still working it out daily. It's who I am.

143

It's the life I live. But it's worth it. I continue to work out those places that need the Master's touch. You know those uncomfortable places in life. We all have them—but somehow, I rise.

I KNOW IT'S MY GOD

Once God broke forth that fountain, that river of life in me to break me free from the power of suicide, I still had residue of my past. It clung to me like a second skin. I knew it because my past interfered with my life. God dealt with me inwardly, continuing to heal old wounds as I surrendered my confused feelings. Knowing that faith is an action word, I had to move toward the plan for my life. I had to trust God. Remember, if I had known how to be free, I wouldn't have been in bondage in the first place.

I had to walk my deliverance out. I still cried and had to stay before God in prayer as He redirected my path. I learned to pray about everything. He showed me which dirty rag to take off next. My "I don't want anybody to know" rag was the worst. Its real name is *pride* and it had to go. Pride is a self-made grave that only you can dig for yourself. Pride always comes before a fall. It's best to be humble.

I am not saying we won't have insecurities to deal with or challenges in life. The difference is, I am no longer on the throne. I can no longer be fulfilled in my desires. My desire has become submitting to His perfect will for my life. Anything less is meaningless. Christ now lives in me.

IS IT REALLY YOUR LIFE?

Can we really live life like we want to? Can we be reckless without thought, with no one to answer to for our decisions, and then think there are no consequences? Eventually, we must answer for how we've lived. I believe the whole Bible and there is a heaven or hell for each one of us. Our life is not our own.

You are the only person who can keep you from a life filled with destruction. You can blame this person or that person, but to find the deliverance you need, you must be honest. Evaluate your life. Determine the good, the bad, and the ugly and actively pursue strengthening the good, improving the bad, and getting rid of the ugly. Accept the Lord's hand when He reaches out to you to save you from drowning in your sin.

If you are in the category of being all right, help someone else become free. My answer was God. Giving my life to the Creator, the One who birthed my life. Without God, I would have no life to call my own. I am talking about a God who can destroy both soul and body (Matthew 10:28).

This is a gift from God. Whether you accept it or not, Jesus Christ's blood was shed for you and me. We were bought with a price. There's power in the blood. Our new name is in the blood. Our forgiven sins are in the blood. Our healing is in the blood, and new life is in the blood. We can live free of masks in the blood.

<u>YOU ARE A GOOD PERSON</u>

You are a good person because of Christ. You even do great things. You are a help to all those around you, but there's still something missing. Can't you hear the call and the sound of life? It's the sound of a good person finding out who they are, by seeing who He is. Good people don't make it to heaven. Saved people do (Romans 10:9-13). It is those who receive Jesus Christ as their personal Savior. Salvation is repenting of your sins, believing that Jesus shed His blood for your sins, and confessing with your mouth that Jesus is Lord. If you haven't done this, let's pray right now. I will pray with you.

<u>MY PRAYER</u>

Father, in the name of Jesus, I come with my sister; I come with my brother before your throne. I pray right now that You surround your child at this moment. Let them sense your presence as they pray this prayer. Let it be real for them, Lord Jesus. As they let the tears flow or feel the peace, let it be done in Jesus' name.

<u>YOUR PRAYER</u>

Lord Jesus, I ask you to come into my life and forgive me of all my sins. I confess my sins before you this day. I denounce Satan and all his works. I confess Jesus as the Lord of my life. Thank you for saving me. I believe with my heart, and I confess with my mouth that you rose from the dead. I am saved. Write my name in the

Lamb's Book of Life. Today is my God-day with the Lord Jesus! I pray this prayer to the Father in the name of Jesus. Amen.

BUT YOU SAY YOU GO TO CHURCH

Attending a church almost killed me. I went every Sunday and yet I almost died in the church. Why? I was going through the motions—feeling good and putting in time. Church does not give me salvation; being the Church gives me salvation. Christ-like is the way. Church is only an aide to help me stay encouraged, but it is God who puts eternal life in the Church. He puts the life in you and me.

YOU HAVE BEEN SAVED FOR YEARS

I was saved. But, I didn't *know* God until years later. I had given my life to Christ and was saved for three years, but I still found myself on the floor in my living room. I was about to make a deal with the devil. I was about to take my own life because I didn't know how to live in Christ.

Living in Christ means I pray to God and read His Word. Greater than all of this, I apply the Word to my life, admitting my faults. Admitting my need for God to save me continuously from myself is the humbling experience that makes Him real. He is the center. He is my life, and He is my way to eternal salvation. Church attendance has nothing to do with it. Living in Christ is about dying daily to me and my desires (Galatians 5:24-25). Knowing that Jesus

147

lived and died for me is my salvation. Receiving Him and allowing Him to live on the inside of me. He is Lord. A lot of people will receive Him, but they won't allow Him to be Lord of their lives.

YOU FEEL WORTHLESS, HELPLESS

My heart goes out to the one who thinks and believes God does not want them because of what they have done. The one who feels helpless and sees no change. I am not talking to the one who does not want any help. This is for the one who does.

When your self-esteem is low, you can't receive the power of a high supreme being—God. The Bible says God knows you, even from the womb (Jeremiah 1:5). He knows all about it, brother. He knows what you did, sister, and God still bids for you to come to Him. Come and feel His love. Come and get your gift. The Lord saw your past, but He's still in your future. Your help is here.

He will restore you to your rightful place. God has the power to wipe the slate clean, canceling out everything that was ever said about you. He will rename you. He will call you His own. God is love. Love covers all things. I pray God's touch of love on you right now in Jesus' name. He's here just for you.

WHO IS THIS GOD?

Who I am is more than just a good person making it in life. When you come to the place where you can't learn anymore, pride takes root. It takes courage to say my life is this way and not what I portray it to be.

I've met some real people who tell it like it is, but in all of that, we still have to see God. There are folks who talk all the time about faith. They tell us everything they know in their heads, but they still don't know God for themselves in their hearts. When you measure where you are next to who God is, things fall into place. This happens because He is God. It's the knowledge of who God is that directs your path. I went to my husband, who is my pastor, and asked him, "Who is God?" After he searched for words to identify this awesome Being, his response was simply, "He is...God."

I was like, "Baby, I know." But how do I put this in words? I could not come up with the words to describe this God I served. I thought about some of the words often used to describe Him like, Everlasting Father. He sits high and looks down low. He is I AM. He is the air we breathe. He is an all-knowing and all-powerful God. He is merciful and just. He is Healer, Master. He is who He is. The All-Supreme Being is God. His name is above all names. All kingdoms know and respond to the name of God.

Jesus asked Peter, "Who do you say that I am?" Peter responded, "Thou are the Christ" (8:27-33). What a power-packed statement. Salvation and deliverance is in Christ. Yokes are destroyed in that name. Christ. The name says it all. It's in the name.

We exist because God has a purpose for us. When we become who God wants us to be, our purpose is manifested. This is what matters. Do you want to know who you are? Find out your purpose in God. My name is not sin. It's Purpose. My identity is not hidden behind a mask. I wear a badge for Christ. God sent His Son, Jesus, that I might be free to reach my destiny.

All those other things fell off as I looked toward God. I found out how to live. I am to live in Christ, being Christ-like in all things.

Do I fall short? You know I do. Do I get it? Because of Him, yes, I do. I keep all imperfections before the throne in my prayer closet. Where is my prayer closet? My car, living room, work desk, at the gym, etc. My prayer closet is wherever I need to call on Him. He's there and everywhere. He is God.

The great I AM is what I need at that very moment. God is all of that for me. Nobody can touch the I AM. It's not in a job, what I do, or anything. It's in Him that I am made complete. When everything else passes away, and it will (Matthew 24:35), God will still be on the throne (Psalm 45:6).

While we search and allow the masks of life to define us, we live on borrowed time. As we think we have nowhere to go, we lose precious time, knowing that silence is not the answer.

God has a place prepared for you. There's room for all who will come. He knows right where you are, and His hand is extended.

Take off the mask, be real, and acknowledge your need for a Father who knows what is best for you. All the hurts, the wrongs done to you, and everything you could have ever done is under the blood of Jesus. You don't have to hide. You don't have to mask.

The gift of life is waiting for you. Will you accept?

'Who shall save me from myself' was my first preached message. The Lord is strong and mighty. He can save you from sin, save you from yourself. He rescued me from myself. He wants to do the same for you. He wants all of me, and He wants all of you. Not just a portion while you keep the rest. All of you. For He gives Himself, this is life to you. In doing so, He makes all His children's benefits available to you. You are an heir to the kingdom.

My God, He's your Alpha and Omega (Revelations 1:8). God is the author; He's the pages in between and the One who declares "The End." He is God, and His love reaches down to you and me daily. Hear the sound? He's calling your name.

UNMASK:

- Take a sheet of paper and write down the negative names you've been called. Write down the negative, nagging thoughts you have about yourself. These are all lies and should be cast away. Take the sheet of paper and tear it into shreds. Throw every piece away.

- Write your name on a sheet of paper. Underneath it, write down every positive word that comes to mind. Write down scriptures. This is who you are. God's creation is good. Walk in the goodness that God created. Place it in your wallet or on your wall so you can refer to it when the lying enemy comes to you. Always declare who you are in Christ Jesus.

Chapter Thirteen
CHANGE YOUR CLOTHES
NEW WARDROBE

❦

When a Samaritan woman came to
draw water, Jesus said to her, "Will
you give me a drink?" His disciples
had gone into the town to buy food
(John 4:7-8).

MY SISTER AT THE WELL . . .

The Lord took time out to zoom in on the woman at the well. It wasn't that she was the only one at the well that day, but it was her hour to change. She knew who Jesus was because she had heard about Him. She broke it down to Him, "You can't be talking to me!" But indeed the Lord was talking to her. "Sir," the woman said, "you have nothing to draw with, and the well is deep. Where can you get this living water" (John 4:11)?

Like us, the woman responded out of her flesh from the perspective of what she knew. She couldn't perceive the living water. She used her logic, not comprehending the spiritual implication of Jesus's words. There is no true satisfaction from the natural elements. Jesus offered her another level. The Lord was getting ready to give her some new taste buds. Just a drink from Him would quench any worldly fire. Jesus answered, "Everyone who drinks this water will be thirsty again, but whoever drinks the living water I give him will never thirst. Indeed, the water I give him will become in him a spring of water welling up to eternal life." The woman said to him, "Sir, give me this water so I won't get thirsty and have to keep coming here to draw water (John 4:13-15).

Even though she didn't quite understand everything Jesus said, her response was, "I want it now." She might have thought to herself, *I will try this one time. Everything else I am doing isn't working. I want to taste this water.*

In my mind, sister girl continued and said, "I don't want to have to come back to this well." In other words, if it's all you say it is, make it so I don't have to come back to my old stomping ground. She wanted a full deliverance.

This woman didn't even realize she was now speaking kingdom language. She was well on her way to a no-turning-back point in her life.

I think about my sister at the well and all the embarrassment she faced. I think about the mistakes she made. I think about all of the people she thought could save her. Oh, how her heart ached. She was in pain. She didn't know what could heal her. She tried everything, and still, she felt empty.

What are you trying to fix in your life? Are you still coming up empty? If so, drink the living water; let the Lord fill your cup.

NO SATISFACTION LIKE JESUS

Sex, no matter how much you get or how good it feels, is only a temporary satisfaction. A kind word spoken gives pleasure. It is music to the ear, but is soon forgotten. Having a man or a woman on your arm is great for your ego, but it's just a covering. It is another mask.

When you are in the wrong place with the wrong people, it is nothing but a waste of time. My sister at the well went through all those men and still ended up alone and broken. She had finally gotten to the place where she found help.

Jesus showed up.

SURE, SHE MESSED UP—SO HAVE WE

In her mind, she was tired of herself, but she couldn't stop. She lived in a familiar place. She did what she knew, doing what she felt she had to do. I don't know who mistreated her or why she didn't feel loved, but God kept her until the appointed time. She was laughed at, scorned, talked about, and maybe slapped in the face for sleeping with somebody's husband. Even at the well, the people criticized her.

But God…

He used it all to make her who she was meant to be.

Her past was not her future. Her mistakes caused her to be merciful to others. She was not like some who acted as if they have never done anything wrong. No, this sister knew there was something better and she met her something better face-to-face.

She got her spiritual thirst quenched at the well with Jesus. The Lord told her everything she had done and who she had done it with, and He still wanted her. No matter her past or her sin she was still one of His ordained women of God. He had a place for her in Him. The Lord told her that when she got a taste of new life, she would hunger for the old no more. One word from Jesus changed the course of her life.

I can't explain why she loved so many men. I don't know why her life went this way. Only she and God knows. I believe she was looking for love on familiar ground, but she didn't look upward.

She fell into learned behavior to survive. The behavior became habit-forming—a stronghold. Her way of life became too great for her to escape on her own. Then, Jesus showed up. One Word from the Lord gave her a shift.

I can relate to this woman being misunderstood. I have done some distasteful things as a means to survive. I have felt the burden of being an outcast. I have seen the hatred from my own community. People mistreated me. Yet, I tried to make it right by pleasing people.

Her adultery was wrong, a symptom of a greater need. It was the only way she knew. It is tempting to conclude that she could have chosen another path. But, how many times have we done the wrong thing when we knew better?

We don't know how this woman grew up or what her mother or other family members had done to her. We don't know what Cousin Sue and Uncle Albert did to shatter her foundation. All I know is that we have a page out of this woman's life. We don't know the entire story. Maybe that's all we need to know. Then we can all relate on some level.

No matter what sin you have committed, sin is sin. We all have gotten dirty. Even little white lies are a sin before God. This woman pressed past what she had become to see more of Jesus.

The more she pursued Jesus, the less she saw herself. This is the place of divine walking in what God created us to be, and not what we have become through the storms we created.

I'm certain as that woman looked back over her life, she saw that she could go back and help somebody else. Why not? In fact, she did when she brought the whole town to Jesus. She already knew shame and how it felt for no one to like her. The sister at the well had nothing to lose and love to gain. What she received was more love than she ever had from her five lovers. This sister—my sister at the well—now had enough love to share with others. Two-thousand years later, we are sharing her testimony. I believe if she could talk to us, the woman at the well would say, "it was all for my making."

Now, let God make you.

UNMASK:

- How do you relate to our sister at the well?

- Have you ever accused anyone without having their story?

- Examine why or how you judged them. Was it harshly? If so, find out why because there's a deeper root.

Chapter Fourteen

CAN JESUS BE REAL IN YOUR LIFE?

B ack in the day, the real church could free any bondage by singing a spiritual hymn over and over as the presence of God filled the temple. With the preached Word, shackles were broken—even off those not looking for freedom. The sheer presence of God nudges at your soul, making you aware of your need for freedom. The power of God was strong, unhindered. The congregation prepared the way. People wept uncontrollably because the love of God touched all who were present. Covered sin was not prevalent because people knew your story and what devil to pray off you. They loved the sinner back to God with power because there was a genuine love for God in the house.

We've heard it before, but some still don't understand to hate the sin, not the sinner. The church should be a place of healing. Unfortunately, in many cases, it is not because *love* is not present. Love must be present for healing to take place.

What has happened to genuine Christian love in the house of God? How do people come in and leave without being changed?

Habits. Rituals. These things allow us to attend church without feeling the presence of God. We go because this is what we are taught, what we are supposed to do. We go weekly but leave the same way we arrive: broken and filled with the shame of our sin. Because of this, we now have those among us who simply don't do church.

In my experience, we do church on Sundays, dropping our sin at the door before we enter. Then, almost immediately, we go back to reclaim the sin we dropped.

I have friends who attend Mass and have no idea what they are doing. I mean literally. I asked a few what this and that meant, and they couldn't tell me. I need to know why I am getting out of bed. It is a lot of work to do something just to say I did it.

It grieves my soul when people come to church expecting to receive love and acceptance, but we fail them. I've been there. Have you?

What's blocking the power? Could it be another scandal brewing from the preacher in the pulpit? A man or woman of God is struggling with sin with no one to talk to and nowhere to go. Yet, they keep preaching as if all is well. No doubt their sin is spilling out onto the people. When people hear unflattering gossip and rumors and begin to stay away, they may also feel as though they have a license to do what the leader is doing.

Could the inability to draw power be because of the "saints" who just left the club, bringing spirits of darkness with them as they come to church? Is it the habit of just coming to Sunday morning worship to feel good? Are we just paying our dues by putting in time, but not wanting to change who we are?

It's almost like we are screaming, "Don't touch my stuff!" You know those types, simply wanting an essay from the preacher, but they won't deal with the Word of God.

What is this? Maybe the church needs another praise team or dance team to entertain, creating a concert-like atmosphere?

I'm reaching. But, what do you think?

Are we hindering the power of God in the church by simply going through the motions of being a Bible-thumping, church goer but not living it? God called us to be doers of the word (James 1:22). There is no power when we do not live out our salvation. Lives do not change when salvation is a word without action.

<u>YOU DON'T NEED ALL OF THIS</u>

People have many reasons for not attending church. I go because of my relationship with God. Some feel they are better off not going because of the drama—perceived or experience. Other times, money—the unwillingness to part with it—will keep us away.

I remember a time when a two dollar offering is all I gave. On a good day, I gave five. They would not mess up my hard-earned money. Once I learned the truth about why we give, my offerings reflected my faith in God to support the church. Yes, some pastors mismanage. But, we either let God deal with them or move our membership to a place God leads us.

Then there are our perceptions that may not be the truth. Success will create the illusion that people don't need God. What you accomplish is not by your strength alone. My friend, God Almighty is the reason you breathe. Without living breath, you cannot do anything. He loves you, even though you don't acknowledge Him. A good life is not the indicator that all is well with your soul. There's Someone we both must answer to when this life is over.

You who are churchgoers and members in good standing, you think you are all right, huh? You don't need all of this because you know the Lord. Well, great. That is wonderful. I am glad to know you have always been real and you treat everybody kind, walking in the love of God. This is a great place to be. But I have a few questions for you.

Are you testifying about the goodness of the Lord?

How many have come to the Lord because of how you live? Not by what you say, but do they come because they saw the hope of you? In other words, does your life always speak salvation? Do others see Christ?

DON'T JUDGE ME!

I heard somebody once say, "If you want to see the biggest hypocrites, go to church." This thing is a two-fold problem. Some people stay away because "church folks" commit the most sins. Sin is sin, so it's not the quantity that is the issue. It's the pointing of fingers while committing the same sins. Lucy Mae was just forgiven and delivered two minutes ago, but she's talking about others as if they are lower than dirt. Didn't she used to do the same thing? Churchgoers can sometimes forget God had to clean them up. *Holier than thou* attitudes cause people to run from the church and God.

What kind of person are you at church?

"At least I go to church." Have you heard that before from family and friends? I have, and I thought it once myself. That was until I found out I hadn't known salvation. I was just a churchgoing, pew warmer. Not to mention, I wasn't about to bring anybody else with me until I got myself right. But going to church is what I knew. I was good at it. I cried at the right places during the service—genuine tears. After emoting, nothing in me changed. We live our lives outside of the church walls. We need to know salvation. To know it is to live it.

Although it's a great place to start, attendance is not enough.

LET'S BE REAL ABOUT IT, FOR JUST A MOMENT

When your sin affects others, you need to take a look at yourself (Matthew 7:3). You don't want to die like this, do you? You say you can't change? Please believe there is a God who has the power to change you.

If you are attending a church that teaches the whole Bible, you can grow. If you are not attending church because of the hypocrites or people you know who say Hallelujah in one breath and swear in the next, I understand. Believe me, I do. I saw them, too, but everyone is not like this. Let me encourage you by telling you the truth. The people who live like that have not known salvation.

True salvation asks and answers:

"Who shall save me from me?"

The Lord strong and mighty shall deliver me from old ways as I allow salvation to touch each part of my life. He is strong enough to deliver us. God is a mighty God (Psalm 24:8).

There's a Clint Brown song that goes, "When all that I am responds to who you are."

That is to know salvation. All that you are, whether good or bad, takes notice of who God is and begin to change. Thus, bringing you and me back to the image we were created to be, a reflection of His love.

When we reflect His love, it brings us to our purpose in Him. We are called to spread the Good News of Jesus Christ and make disciples of the nations (Matthew 28:19).

IT'S TIME TO PULL BACK THE COVERS

We play God when we attempt to hide and cover our sin. Jesus is love and love covers a multitude of sin (I Peter 4:8). He died so we don't have to hide because of fear. The Lord Jesus is our cover. No longer should we build our foundation on covering up heaps, but by taking them to a God who is more than willing to break the yoke. The church should magnify the love of God by allowing people to be free and real in the presence of God, in a holy sanctuary.

The church will never be filled with perfect people, but it should be filled with the power of a perfect, loving God, the power to break pride and bring about humility. Walking with Christ causes us to love, not criticize. We must meet the needs of the people we encounter. We must receive and love them by making room for them to come in and fellowship. We should raise the bar for holiness because Jesus is the standard.

If you are a believer, the individuals that cross your path should not feel judgment. Jesus taught in love. Let your countenance reflect His love. People should know there is a God who will love them right now, right where they are. Just the same way He first loved you, remember? When you receive forgiveness, you must use that to extend love to the next person.

<u>TO MY SISTERS</u>

We have tolerated sin in our homes, in our children, and in our relationships. We enable others, allowing them to drain us. Like the woman at the well, we have been misunderstood, misused, and misled. We have loved the wrong man. We have allowed the bruises from our pasts to dictate our futures.

These things have caused our hearts to bleed. We have cried tears that only God knows about. Each step and turn we made, God saw us. Remember to let go and let God. Come out of hiding. Walk your walk. Walk it out.

The butterfly you have become, the woman you are today, and the essence of who you are is what makes you special. You made it, now let God keep making you. With our hair done and nails manicured, we feel pretty. This is good. However, the true beauty is when you and I have the makeup of His glory. Then and only then are we so beautiful that lost and hurt people notice. You are a beacon of hope and love for other women.

<u>TO MY BROTHERS</u>

It's not in the moves between the sheets that make you a man. That's a message my husband consistently ministers to men. It's what you do in God that will make you strong. Stand against all the odds, but be strong enough to bow your heart to a Holy God. Surrendering to God is a characteristic of a man who has everything. Find everything that you lack or need in God.

It takes courage to respond to God's touch in your life.

And, you need healing from yesterday. You don't have to survive the world's way. God is the right way. Know your name. Your name does not respond to destruction—your name is Kingdom. Let go of anger and abusive ways, and lay it all at the altar before God. You can find freedom in Christ because you are strong enough to say, "I need Thee, oh Lord." A well-groomed man who is geared up for life is always a plus. But a man who loves the Lord is so much greater, so much finer.

TO MY PASTORS OR LEADERS

Don't let your secret keep you from your true destiny. It isn't worth it. Isn't it detrimental to hold on to something that has the potential to destroy what God has used you to build? Please don't keep operating in a role because of the unknown or because of what others might think. It's time for you to be free from yokes. Free from lust and adultery. Free from anger and abuse. Free from addictions. Free from porn. Free from pride. You know your sin and so does God. How long must He tarry with you? Don't let the devil keep naming you (Psalms 51:6).

I know you feel like there's no one to share your struggle. Go to the one who sees all. God is waiting.

He ordained you. He chose you. Choose Him so you can fulfill your purpose. Opening your mouth before Him will cause the river to flow once again. I know your deepest desire is to be free. Secrets have a way of seeping out. Get the situation before God. He will see you through. He knew what you would face, and He knew where you would fall. God's grace is sufficient. It's more than enough to see you through any obstacle of life. The power is the secret. Break the curse.

<u>YOU CAN'T CHANGE THEM</u>

Neither you nor I have the power to change the church or people in general. Humans are flawed. That's just how it is. But we do have the power to change who we are and what we have become. We can lift someone or tear them down by the very thing we allow to dictate our movement. I pray that God is the orchestrator of your movement.

Life is busy, but we must take notice. If we are not careful and observant, we will miss the Bethany's all around us. Or worse, if God is not our life, we may become Bethany as we become numb to life.

I encourage you to press through all the obstacles and those things that try to name you and DECLARE WHO YOU ARE. There's only One who can name you. Believe that God will direct your path if you trust Him to.

I honestly don't know how I would make it without God being in my life. It's what I have become. It's what I do. I strive to be the best me I know how to be. I've told you before, I fall short, but my name has changed. I challenge you to try God. Try on the name He gave you.

God is life unto us. Know God and know you. See God and be you. If you are unmasked, living in truth, then all you do will reflect God. Your life will sing the melody, "All that I am, is because of who you are."

UNMASK:

- Listen to the words you speak. Pay attention because it's a reflection of your life. How are the words you speak a reflection of your life?

- In what way does your words contradict the life you actually live?

- What actions reflect the true you? How will you change?

- When will you begin?

Author Postscript

O ne of the barriers to me telling my story was how it would affect my parents. I never wanted anyone to think they knew and did nothing. The only reason I didn't tell them is that I knew they would do something to the people hurting me.

As I mentioned in Chapter Eight, my mother found out about my abuse through my angry ex-boyfriend. He may have meant well, but his response wasn't what my mother or I needed. It felt horrible to watch my mother battle with the hurt, anger and disappointment of the situation.

Even with the door open to expose my abusers, I didn't share the details with my parents until the first edition of *Who I Become* hit the bookshelves.

It wasn't the best way.

But, in my defense, even after I told Tony all of the ins and outs, my complete healing didn't come until I wrote this book. It was surreal. As details resurrected effortlessly onto the pages, they flowed like water being poured into a tall glass. As I meet with women who have their stories, I tell them to journal what happened to them. It's a positive outlet, and I wish I had done that sooner. The story has to come **up** and **out** of the heart. Then the real work of healing becomes activated.

My dad is not one to pick up a book and read, but I insisted he read the book before I published it. I'm telling you, I heard about it. I will never forget the day my dad called me at work, and I squeaked out, "Daddy...I'm sorry..." in response to his question, "Why didn't you tell me?" *The least I could do* was hold the phone as he vented and asked question after question. Today, my dad has forgiven those who trespassed against his baby girl, agreeing it was probably best he didn't know at the time. I knew what he meant. Back then my dad didn't know the Lord. Who knows what would have happened?

I never meant to hurt anyone with my silence, but I did. I thought I was protecting us all. I have heard others tell me how crushed they were because their parents didn't believe them. Thankfully, mine did.

We all have different endings.

Only my sisters and a close friend were my confidants because we all had kept secrets that we silently swore would go to our graves. But God had a different story.

Since the first release of this book, a few family members who don't agree with me airing my laundry before the world decided to confront me. It stung to hear them come at me like they did. The silent treatment isn't fun to endure. Nevertheless, God has me on assignment. If my dirty laundry cleans someone else's stains, it's all worth it. TruU Ministries was birthed out of *Who I've Become*. Even though I experienced some negativity from writing and publishing this book, I had those that came, one by one, and said, "It happened to me, too." Some had not told a soul, but after reading my story, they opened up their vaults to tell the truth. Some of these women had forgotten what happened and often wondered why they acted this way and that. Now they knew why and it allowed the tears they hadn't even known existed to flow. Breaking my silence was worth it. My story, this book, and my ministry help others because God is in the midst. God is listening to the soul cries and healing waters will soothe the withered souls.

Your healing is first and foremost about you and your relationship with God. Through Him not only will you find deliverance, healing, and the TruU, you will begin to build stronger relationships with the people God placed in your life.

About the Author

Known for dealing with controversial topics within the church community, Sonya Visor is an author, an inspirational "keep-it-real" speaker, a playwright and the founder of TruU Ministries, which was birthed from her inspirational book, Who I've Become. Sonya writes and ministers to help people become the true person God ordained them to be. Helping people unmask to reveal their true self is not only Sonya's passion but also the mantle of deliverance she lives and walks in.

When Sonya is not busy writing or ministering, she enjoys spending time with her better half, reading, watching a great movie and baking chocolate chip cookies.

Sonya resides in Wisconsin with her husband of over twenty-five years, Pastor Tony, and their two sons. Sonya and her husband pastor New Covenant Church, Racine.

Readers can connect with Sonya online and join the Unapologetically TruU FaceBook Community:

Sonyavisor.com | Facebook.com/sonya.visor | Twitter.com/sonyavisor |

•Pinterest.com/unmask1• Goodreads

Sonya at sonya@sonyavisor.com and find more books by visiting her website at www.sonyavisor.com

SIGN UP VIA EMAIL FOR FREE DOWN LOADABLE
WHO I'VE BECOME

STUDY GUIDE

VISIT WWW.SONYAVISOR.COM